EVALUATING EDUCATIONAL RESEARCH

Gordon Edward Fuchs
University of Dayton

University Press
of America™

Library of Congress Catalog Card Number: 80-5480

To my wife, Joanne; our sons,
Paul Joseph; Stephen Matthew;
Mark Andrew; Philip Edward;
Anthony James; and my parents,
Jacob and Helen.

iii

ACKNOWLEDGEMENTS

Many people have supported me in this endeavor, and I would like to thank each for his or her contribution. Thanks to:

Herman Torge and Bernard Harawa who read the manuscript and offered many valuable suggestions.

Ellis Joseph who provided moral and financial assistance.

Simon Chavez who first introduced me to the concept of "consumer of research".

John O'Donnell and members of the University's Sabbatical Leave Committee who granted me a sabbatical in order to work on this project.

John Geiger who used his wit to help relieve my self-imposed pressures.

Rita Schmidt, my former secretary, who typed parts of the first manuscript.

Susan Utrup, my present secretary, who spent endless hours typing and proofreading.

Colleen Wildenhaus who spent many hours typing the final manuscript. All three of the women mentioned above endured many demands imposed by this project.

I hope that I have not forgotten anyone. Any omission is not intentional.

TABLE OF CONTENTS

PREFACE

"I never liked reading research. It is too boring."

"I cannot understand research articles. After all, I am just a primary teacher."

"I get confused when I read anything to do with statistics. I never liked math."

These are typical comments expressed by students when confronted with the task of reading and evaluating research studies. Such terms as ".05 level," "significant finding," "null hypothesis," "survey study," etc., tend to mystify them.

It is unfortunate that many education students possess this attitude toward research because such a feeling prevents them from learning fascinating and important information. Many graduate and some undergraduate programs or courses in education require that students read, understand, and evaluate the research in a given area. Knowledge and understanding of research is crucial if educational practitioners and future practitioners hope to be able to evaluate educational research. Such a skill is necessary if professional educators wish to do a better job of teaching students.

This text, Evaluating Educational Research, has been written for the consumer of educational research. Through the presentation of the content and exercises, it is the author's sole purpose to help the reader understand, analyze, and evaluate research.

This text consists of five chapters: Understanding Types of Research, Understanding Hypothesis Testing and Level of Significance, Understanding and Analyzing Historical Research, Understanding and Analyzing Experimental Research, and Evaluating Research. Each chapter is followed by a set of exercises.   The answers to the exercises are given.

If the reader, as a consumer of educational research, takes the time to read and study the material, he should be able to apply these skills to research studies. This feeling of accomplishment should help the consumer of research gain a more positive attitude toward research.

GEF
Dayton, Ohio
April, 1980

CHAPTER ONE

UNDERSTANDING TYPES OF RESEARCH

Many journals in the field of education are
available to professional educators. Some journals
are pedagogically oriented; others are devoted
exclusively to research. Some journals contain
both methods and research articles.

When one reads a methods article, it is
necessary for him to understand the specialized
vocabulary used. Knowledge of the vocabulary will
enable him to comprehend what he is reading. For
example, if a teacher reads a methods article in
the <u>Arithmetic Teacher</u> on the teaching of sets,
the mastery of such terms as finite, infinite,
subset, intersection, union, etc., helps the
teacher to grasp what is written.

Mastery of terminology is also necessary when
one reads research studies which appear in such
sources as professional journals, unpublished
documents, microfiche, etc. This knowledge helps
the teacher as a consumer of educational research
to comprehend what is written.

The purpose of this first chapter is to discuss and explain types of educational research.
After the student has read the chapter, studied
the material, and completed the exercises, he
should be able to:

1. Define the term research,

2. Recall, define, give an example of,
    and identify in a problem situation
    the three major types of research,

3. Recall, define, give an example of,
    and identify in a problem situation
    the three types of applied research,
    and

1

4. Recall, define, give an example of,
    and identify in a problem situation
    five types of descriptive research.

Read the fictional account of the activities
for five different people.

Dr. Smith is a psychologist. He has been
experimenting in his laboratory with rats. Dr.
Smith is trying to find out why rats quarrel and
fight when certain weather conditions are present.
After years of formulating hypotheses, observing,
collecting and analyzing data, etc., Dr. Smith
postulates the theory that on hot, humid, and
muggy days, the rats fight and quarrel more with
one another than they do on days when these atmospheric conditions are not present. Dr. Smith
presents his finding in the form of a theory which
states that the behavior of rats is influenced by
atmospheric conditions.

Mr. Brown is a research specialist for a
large public school system. The school board has
asked him to gather data from the public concerning
its attitude toward the schools. Some of the steps
involved with Mr. Brown's investigation include
stating a problem statement, planning a procedure
that will be used to carry out the problem statement, and collecting and analyzing the data.
After the investigation Mr. Brown concludes that
the public has a laissez-faire attitude toward the
public schools.

Miss Blue is a third grade teacher. Questions
concerning the most efficient way to organize the
learning day have been puzzling her for several
years. After formulating a problem statement,
carrying out a procedure, collecting and analyzing
the data, etc., Miss Blue devises a workable approach on the best way to organize the learning
day.

A graduate student, Mr. Ace, has a deep interest in the history of curriculum development in the United States. He, like Miss Blue, has read extensively in this area. Through his reading he has discovered that curriculum cycles exist, that is, curriculum history tends to repeat itself. Mr. Ace devises a developmental pattern concerning the history of curriculum which describes this phenomenon.

Dr. Jones, a college professor, has read about Dr. Smith's experiments in a research journal. He is fascinated by the theory that Dr. Smith has postulated. He decides to test Dr. Smith's theory with students by designing an experiment to collect data on the behavior of children with respect to different atmospheric conditions. He selects several classrooms in which to conduct his research. After he has stated a problem, developed a hypothesis, collected and analyzed his data, etc., he concludes that varying atmospheric conditions have an effect on children's behavior.

Which of the above persons was involved with conducting research? Was it Dr. Smith? After all, he studied a problem in a laboratory setting. Was it Dr. Jones? He is a college professor and they are supposed to be research oriented. Could Miss Blue's work be considered research? She attempted to solve a problem of significance only to her. What about the efforts of Mr. Ace and Mr. Brown? Were they involved with research?

Actually all of the persons described above were involved with research. In order to understand why people with such divergent backgrounds could possibly be considered researchers, it is necessary to understand what research is.

Research Defined

What is research? Research is a planned and systematic method of collecting and analyzing data in order to solve a problem or to answer a question.

What are the major categories of research? Best (1977) and Shaver (1979) state that there are three basic types: pure, applied and action. This classification will be used as the basis for this discussion.

Pure Research

Pure research is that which has as its goal the discovery of knowledge for the purpose of formulating a theory. Usually this type of research is done in a laboratory where the researcher has rigid control over all the variables. In the examples cited above, Dr. Smith was involved with pure research. He conducted his research in a laboratory where he was able to exercise strict control over all the variables such as temperature, humidity, diet, water, etc.

Criticism toward pure research has been advanced by some segments in the educational community. They feel that the discovery of knowledge in order to formulate a theory may be useless because the theory has little or no practical value. They fail to understand that the primary aim of this research is to discover knowledge so that theories can be formulated; it is the task of the applied researcher to test the theory in a field setting.

Applied Research

The second major category of research is applied research. Applied research is that which has as its goal the testing of a theory or the studying of issues which have a relationship to contemporary problems. It is conducted in a

field setting such as a local community or school.
In the above examples, Dr. Jones conducted applied
research because he tested Dr. Smith's theory in
a field situation. Mr. Brown and Mr. Ace also
conducted applied research. Mr. Brown determined
the public's attitude toward a contemporary problem
while Mr. Ace was able to develop sound conclusions
which could be used to explain why certain conditions affecting curriculum are in vogue today.

Applied research is generally recognized as
consisting of three subtypes: historical,
descriptive and experimental. Historical research
is defined as that kind of research which describes
what was, descriptive research describes what is,
and experimental research is concerned with that
which will happen. (For a thorough account of the
three types of research, see Best, 1977, or Van
Dalen, 1979.)

Historical Research

In the examples in the beginning of this
chapter, Mr. Ace was involved with historical
research. He wanted to study the past so that he
could construct the history of curriculum development. Such information has value because knowledge
of curriculum development can be useful to those
who make curriculum decisions. What worked or did
not work and the reasons why could help educators
make more informed decisions.

Another example of historical research is a
study conducted by Griffin (1968) who wanted to
learn why certain topics are taught in an advanced
high school mathematics class and defend as valid
the use of the historical approach to the teaching of high school mathematics.

In another historical study, Perkins (1967)
studied the work of a group of nuns during the
Civil War. She wanted to relate the story of
these nuns by reconstructing the past. Such a
story has historical merit because it gives the

5

reader an insight into the past.

Descriptive Research

Another major category of applied research is descriptive research. The major intent of this kind of research is to describe what is.

Types of descriptive research are: survey, developmental, case study, correlation and ex post facto.

Survey Research

Survey research is defined as a type of descriptive research which has as its major intent the gathering of opinions about a subject. The well known Gallup Poll is an example of such a study. By carefully selecting a representative group (sample) and gathering and analyzing opinions from the sample, the pollsters can infer how the population feels toward an issue by generalizing the results from the sample. (See Chapter Four for a discussion on sampling techniques.)

Another example of a survey study is a study completed by Hammill (1972). In this study she used a questionnaire to gather the opinions of high school students toward the study of mathematics. Since all of the students in the high school were polled, their collective opinion is representative of students in that school; these results cannot be generalized to other high schools.

In another survey study, Brand (1968) wanted to identify what factors would affect the passage or failure of school tax levies in Ohio. After Brand collected and analyzed his data, he was able to identify the pertinent factors associated with this topic.

A nationwide survey study was completed by Jones and Steinbrink (1977). In this survey they gathered information pertinent to precollege energy education curriculum from representatives in all the states.

Well organized and conducted survey studies are valuable because they give information on a group's attitude toward a topic. Such information can be useful to those involved with planning and evaluating.

Longitudinal Research

Longitudinal research is another type of descriptive research. A longitudinal study is one in which an investigator examines and analyzes the same group or unit over a long period of time in order to determine patterns and sequences of development.

An example of a longitudinal study is a study by Lefkowitz, Eron, Walder and Huesmann (1977). The authors studied the development of aggression. Data was collected from 875 third graders and ten years later additional data was gathered from 436 of the original group. Based on this evidence compiled over a period of time, the authors explained their theory of the development of aggression.

Intensive longitudinal studies were conducted by Gesell (1940) and by Gesell and Ilg (1946). In both studies, children were examined at different time intervals to determine their growth patterns and characteristics. From the data collected, Gesell was able to describe the pattern of development of children during the first five years and from the information compiled by Gesell and Ilg, growth patterns of children from five to ten were stated.

Case Study

A case study is another type of descriptive research. The major objective of a case study is to study a unit in depth in order to understand how the unit functions in its setting.

A case study which involved a whole case was done by Ousley (1978). In this research she analyzed in depth the reading problems of second grade children. In another study, Prah (1965) compiled a picture on the traits of six second grade students with Appalachian background to gain insight as to why they failed. Information gained from studies like these can help researchers to understand how a person or group behaves in its setting.

Correlation Study

Correlation study is another type of descriptive study. In this type of study, the researcher investigates the degree of relationship between phenomena or variables. Information obtained from these types of studies may be used to understand and predict relationships. (See Chapter Two for more discussion about variables.)

An example of a correlation study is one conducted by Fuchs (1961). In this study, the investigator wanted to determine the degree of relationship between the rank ordering of teacher traits and grade level of students. He hypothesized that seventh graders desire different rank order of qualities in an ideal teacher than do ninth graders. A positive correlation would suggest that the compared groups desired a similar rank order of qualities while a negative correlation would point out that the compared groups desired a different ranking of qualities.

Another example of a correlation study is one completed by Doucette and St. Pierre (1977). In this investigation, the authors analyzed the

8

relationship between reading achievement and classroom, school, and pupil variables.

Williams (1968) studied the relationship between two variables: creativity and personality. In this correlational study, he found no relationship between the variables. This finding has value to those who study relationships of this nature.

Correlation studies can also be used as predictive guides. An example of such a study is one conducted by Leahy (1964). In this study Leahy wanted a device which could be useful in predicting college success of graduates from a local high school. She computed a correlation coefficient based on ACT scores (present event) and grades received in college.

In another correlation study, Gaver and Richards (1979) developed an instrument which proved to be useful in predicting achievement differences. Instruments developed in both of these studies can be employed as predictive tools.

Ex Post Facto Study

Another type of descriptive study is the ex post facto study. In this type of research, the investigator is faced with a current problem and tries to determine what caused the problem by examining and searching data in retrospect for possible causes.

Freed (1948) conducted a study to determine the causes of reading failure in a school system. In another study, Mardis (1949) examined causes of school failure in a large school. In both studies, the causes for failure were identified and recommendations were suggested.

Another example of an ex post facto study is one completed by Lazar (1977). In this investigation, he studied the academic success of youngsters enrolled in preschool programs which were initiated in the 1960's in order to discover if such programs enhanced achievement. At the time of his investigation, these children ranged in age from nine to 18 years. Results from a study of this nature can be extremely important for those involved with early childhood education programs.

All of the descriptive studies cited above were conducted in a systematic fashion. Usually each investigator generated a problem statement, reviewed the literature, discussed a methodology for carrying out the problem, compiled results, and suggested recommendations or reached a conclusion. In some of the studies, the researchers generated a hypothesis. If a hypothesis is written, it must be related to the problem statement.

Experimental Research

Another type of applied research is experimental research. Experimental research is research in which a theory or problem is analyzed by studying cause and effect relationships. An independent variable(s) is manipulated to study its effect upon a dependent variable(s).

An independent variable is the treatment, experimental, or manipulated variable. A dependent variable is the outcome variable. If a researcher wishes to determine the effectiveness of using a certain method of reading on achievement of students, the independent variable is the method of teaching reading and the dependent variable is the gain or loss in achievement. (See Chapter Two for more discussion on variables.)

Puhak (1977) conducted an experimental study in her classroom. She wanted to determine the effects of reading aloud to children on vocabulary development. In another experimental study,

10

Kolesar (1973) studied the effects of four different types of praise on the self concept of primary pupils. In both studies, the method of presentation was the independent variable. The dependent variable was the achievement score. Since cause and effect relationships were examined, these studies are experimental ones.

Another example of an experimental study is one completed by De Medio (1979). In this study, De Medio compared two methods of teaching French culture to French students to determine which approach produced more growth in listening, speaking, reading, and writing skills. De Medio also wished to find out what approach produced positive attitudes toward the French people.

The experimental studies mentioned so far were executed in a systematic fashion. The researcher stated the problem, generated a hypothesis, reviewed the literature, devised the procedures, analyzed the data and reached a conclusion.

Action Research

Action research is another major category of research. Action research is research aimed at the solving of a problem in a local setting such as the classroom. The researcher, often a classroom teacher, is not interested in generalizing his results to other settings nor is he concerned with the rigid controls of variables. In the examples used in the beginning of the chapter, Miss Blue was involved with this type of research.

An example of such a study is one conducted by Jenkins (1967). As a special education teacher, she felt that it was necessary to develop instruments (measuring devices) to aid teachers in measuring, recording and reporting the progress of slow learning pupils.

11

A study by Bowers (1967) is another example of action research. In his study, he devised a flexible schedule for a middle school because prior schedules failed to work.

Still another example of action research is a study completed by Johnson (1970). Johnson, faced with a lack of materials for the non reader, devised creative activities for her students.

In the studies by Jenkins, Bowers, and Johnson, each investigator was confronted with a problem of concern to that individual. This condition plus the fact that no one was concerned with controlling variables or generalizing results qualify these studies as examples of action research.

When a person conducts action research, he also goes through a systematic process. He needs to state the problem, review the literature, describe how he will solve the problem, determine his results, and reach a conclusion.

In this chapter, the definition of research was presented. Also mentioned were the major types of research, three kinds of applied research, and five types of descriptive research.

It is not always easy to categorize research as a distinct type. Sometimes research may involve elements from two or more types. This type of study is called an eclectic study.

An example of an eclectic kind of research is a study done by Fangman (1973). In this study, Fangman determined the degree of relationship between scores on the Illinois Test of Psycholinguistic Ability and teacher ratings for reading readiness. The correlation coefficient was used to predict readiness for reading. Because characteristics of two studies are present, this is classified as a correlation-predictive study.

Another example of an eclectic type of study is one completed by Roettger, Szymczuk and Millard (1979). In this study the authors validated a reading attitude scale and used this scale to study the relationship between attitude and reading achievement. This study can be classified as a validation-correlation study.[1]

To be able to distinguish between the different types of research enables the consumer of research to better understand and analyze research types.

_____

[1]A validation study such as the one cited above is one in which a measuring instrument is tested to determine its usefulness.

EXERCISES -- CHAPTER ONE

Directions: Complete the following exercises.
The answers are given at the end of the exercises.

1. Define and give an example of each of the
   following.

   a. Pure Research _____

   _____

   _____

   _____

   b. Applied Research _____

   _____

   _____

   _____

   c. Action Research _____

   _____

   _____

   _____

   d. Define the term research _____

   _____

   _____

2. You are concerned about the attitudes of your eighth graders toward the use of drugs. In order to find out what they are thinking, you administer a questionnaire to them.

   a. What kind of study is this? _____

   _____

   b. Why? _____

   _____

3. You are interested in learning how instructional strategies changed and evolved during the last 200 years. You conduct an intensive search of the literature and discover when and how this concept originated.

   a. What kind of study is this? _____

   _____

   b. Why? _____

   _____

4. You notice some of your third grade students have a good attitude toward school while others have a poor attitude toward school. You decide to investigate the reasons for this condition. Your investigation includes the years your children first entered school up to the present.

   a. What kind of study is this? _____

   _____

   b. Why? _____

   _____

5. You feel that you need to devise a different
    approach to the teaching of spelling. You are
    concerned only with solving this problem and
    you have no intention of generalizing your
    results or controlling all variables.

    a. What type of study is this? _____

        _____

    b. Why? _____

        _____

6. You ask two of your colleagues to help you
    determine if the A method of teaching spelling
    produces higher achievement than the B method.
    You design your experiment so that you can
    control as many of the variables as possible.

    a. What type of study is this? _____

        _____

    b. Why? _____

        _____

7. You wish to study the mental characteristics
    of children over a five year period. Five
    thousand children, all age one month, are
    included. Every three months you study how
    the children have grown mentally.

    a. What type of study is this? _____

        _____

    b. Why? _____

        _____

8. You wish to study the relationship between diet and school achievement.

   a. What type of study is this? _____

      _____

   b. Why? _____

      _____

9. You wish to do an in depth study of your class. Most of the children have emotional problems, and you want to determine how the class functions within the school.

   a. What kind of study is this? _____

      _____

   b. Why? _____

      _____

17

ANSWERS TO EXERCISES FOR CHAPTER ONE

1a. Pure research is research that has as its goal the discovery of knowledge or the formation of a theory. Example -- open ended answer.

1b. Applied research is research which has as its goal the testing of a theory or the studying of issues which have a relationship to present problems. Example -- open ended answer.

1c. Action research is research aimed at the solving of a problem in a local setting such as the classroom. Example -- open ended answer.

1d. Research is a planned and systematic method of collecting data in order to solve a problem or to answer a question.

2a. Survey.

2b. You ask their opinion toward a topic.

3a. Historical.

3b. You examine the past in order to explain the development of a concept.

4a. Ex post facto.

4b. You are faced with a current problem and you examine and search data in retrospect for possible causes.

5a. Action.

5b. You solve a present problem in the setting of the classroom.

6a. Experimental.

6b. You manipulate the independent variable (method) to determine the outcome (achievement).

7a. Longitudinal.

7b. You are studying a phenomenon over a long period of time.

8a. Correlation.

8b. You wish to determine the degree of relationship between the two variables: diet and school achievement.

9a. Case study.

9b. You study one unit in depth to see how it functions in its setting.

CHAPTER TWO

UNDERSTANDING HYPOTHESIS TESTING AND LEVEL OF SIGNIFICANCE

Many times when the consumer of educational research reads the literature he will note that the researcher generated a hypothesis. A hypothesis is always related to the statement of the problem, and it serves to provide the researcher with a tentative or probable solution to the problem. The researcher will then test the hypothesis to determine if he should reject or not reject it.

The purpose of this chapter is to discuss and explain certain key concepts related to hypothesis testing. After the student has read this chapter, studied the material, and completed the exercises, he should be able to:

1. Define the following terms:

   a. Independent variable,
   b. Dependent variable,
   c. Null hypothesis,
   d. Pre- and posttest, and
   e. Type I and Type II error.

2. Identify both types of variables in a problem situation,

3. State under what conditions the null hypothesis is rejected or not rejected (accepted),

4. State what is meant when the null hypothesis is rejected or not rejected (accepted), and

5. State what is meant by a designated level of significance.

Paul S. Philips is a teacher of mathematics. Two years ago, he taught the concept of subtraction which involved regrouping of two place whole numbers (example: 61 - 39) by using a deductive or expository teaching strategy. This strategy involved showing and telling the students how to solve such problems. Although Mr. Philips noticed that his children learned the concepts, he was not satisfied with the overall achievement of the class.

Last year Mr. Philips decided to teach this concept by employing an inductive teaching strategy. He used teacher questions to help the children discover how to solve problems of this nature. He was more satisfied with the achievement of the children when this approach was used than he was when he used the deductive approach.

This year Mr. Philips does not know which approach to use. His class obtained higher test results when he used the inductive approach, but he does not know if the results are due to the superiority of the method or uncontrolled factors which affected the results. To help Mr. Philips determine which approach is more effective, he decided to conduct a study in his classroom in which he hopes to determine which method will produce a significant finding in achievement.

Null Hypothesis

As part of Mr. Philips's study, he generates a statement which states that there is no significant difference in mean gain achievement scores of fifth grade students who are taught a mathematical concept (regrouping in subtraction) using the deductive approach when compared to a similar group which is taught the same concept using the inductive approach.

The above statement is referred to as the null hypothesis (symbol: H_o). Sometimes it is called the hypothesis of no difference, the statistical hypothesis, or the nondirectional hypothesis. The null hypothesis simply means that there is no significant difference between the phenomena under study. In this example the null hypothesis states that there is no significant difference between the mean gain scores of the two groups.

After Mr. Philips has written the null hypothesis, he randomly divides his class of 30 students into two equal groups. He decides to teach Group A the regrouping concept by using the inductive method; Group B is taught the same concept by the deductive approach. He lists the names of the children and randomly assigns the method to each group. In Figure 2.1 are the names of the children in each group.

Group A (N = 15)   Group B (N = 15)

        Inductive   Deductive

    1. Daniel   1. Mary
    2. Janice   2. Anthony
    3. Jerry   3. Susan
    4. Alice   4. Paul
    5. Tom   5. Helen
    6. Marilyn   6. Stephen
    7. Chris   7. Marie
    8. Linda   8. Mark
    9. David   9. Nancy
   10. Carol   10. Philip
   11. George   11. Judy
   12. Melissa   12. John
   13. Eugene   13. Anne
   14. Barbara   14. Jack
   15. Howard   15. Joanne

    Figure 2.1. The names of the fifteen children in the inductive group are listed in the left hand column. The names of the children in the deductive group are listed in the right hand column. N stands for sample size.

23

Mr. Philips decides to conduct the experiment
for four weeks. He plans to give a pretest (a test
given before an experiment is conducted) to the
children in each group, teach the concept by using
the inductive approach with Group A and the deductive approach with Group B for a period of four
weeks, and administer a posttest (a test given
after an experiment is conducted) to the children
in each group. See Figure 2.2. By comparing each
child's pretest with his posttest, he can determine
the amount of positive or negative gain in achievement for each child.

Pretests	Teaches Concept Using	Posttests
Group A	Inductive Approach	Group A
Pretests	Teaches Concept Using	Posttests
Group B	Deductive Approach	Group B

Figure 2.2. The three stages of the
experiment for each group.

Below in Figure 2.3 are pretest and posttest
results along with the gain achievement score for
each child.[1] The highest possible score for either
test is ten.

---

[1]Whether or not gain or change scores should
be used to measure the outcome of the experiment
has to be decided by the researcher. Best (1977),
Van Dalen (1979), and Isaac (1971), all seem to
imply that such a procedure is acceptable. Kennedy
(1978), feels the use of such scores presents problems. He suggests three alternative procedures one
can employ to cope with this problem. See also Lord
(1956), McNemar (1959), Cronbach and Furby (1970),
and Marks and Martin (1973).

24

Inductive

Student	Pretest Score	Posttest Score	Gain Score
1. Daniel	0	8	+8
2. Janice	3	10	+7
3. Jerry	1	9	+8
4. Alice	2	0	-2
5. Tom	2	8	+6
6. Marilyn	0	7	+7
7. Chris	0	8	+8
8. Linda	1	10	+9
9. David	2	9	+7
10. Carol	1	10	+9
11. George	1	10	+9
12. Melissa	3	9	+6
13. Eugene	0	8	+8
14. Barbara	2	10	+8
15. Howard	1	9	+8

Deductive

Student	Pretest Score	Posttest Score	Gain Score
1. Mary	0	2	+2
2. Anthony	1	2	+1
3. Susan	0	0	0
4. Paul	2	1	-1
5. Helen	2	4	+2
6. Stephen	1	3	+2
7. Marie	0	1	+1
8. Mark	3	1	-2
9. Nancy	7	5	-2
10. Philip	0	4	+4
11. Judy	1	3	+2
12. John	3	4	+1
13. Anne	2	0	-2
14. Jack	2	3	+1
15. Joanne	1	2	+1

The mean ($\bar{X}$) gain for the 15 students using the inductive approach = 7.07 and the mean ($\bar{X}$) gain for the 15 students using the deductive approach =.67.

Figure 2.3. Names, pretest, posttest, and gain scores for each of the 30 children. The symbol for the mean score (arithmetical average) is $\bar{X}$.

Notice that some students (Alice, Paul, Mark, Nancy and Anne) scored lower on the posttest than they did on the pretest; therefore, each registered a negative (minus) gain score.

Types of Variables

In this example, two variables can be identified: the independent and dependent. The independent variable is the experimental or manipulated variable. The teaching method is the independent variable because that variable is being manipulated to see what effect it has on achievement. The dependent variable is referred to as the outcome variable. It expresses the outcome of the experimental or independent variable. In this example, the dependent variable is the achievement score of the children.

Up to this point, Mr. Philips has stated his null hypothesis, identified the variables, and designed the experiment. He has also computed the mean gain score for each group. Now Mr. Philips needs to determine whether or not he should reject or not reject his null hypothesis.

Level of Significance

Before discussing when to reject or not reject the null hypothesis, it is necessary to understand what is meant by a designated level of significance.

The symbol p is commonly used to indicate the level of significance. In this example, the .05 level of significance is used because this level is commonly used in educational and psychological research. This means that the probability is five or less out of 100 that the difference is due to chance or sampling error. If the finding is not due to chance or sampling error, something other than chance or sampling error is responsible for producing the result. A level of .001 means that the probability is one or less out of 1000 that the difference is due to chance or sampling error. A finding which is significant at this level is highly significant.

Return to the example in Figure 2.3 and notice that the mean gain score for the deductive group is .67 while the mean gain score for the inductive group is 7.07. By comparing only these mean gain scores, some people might reject the null hypothesis and conclude that a significant finding exists between the two means because one mean gain score is much greater than the other. They would further conclude that the inductive approach to teaching is better than the deductive approach. This is not necessarily the case.

In order to determine if one should reject or fail to reject (accept)[1] the null hypothesis, one needs to compare two numbers. The first number the researcher computes; the second number is found in a statistical table and associated with a predetermined level of significance. In this example Mr. Philips computes a statistical test called the t test. The results of this computation give him the observed or computed value. The computed value

---

[1]Some authorities in the area of research, including Isaac (1971), state that one does not accept the null hypothesis. One fails to reject it.

27

of t is 7.8 with 28 degrees of freedom (d.f.). (It is not necessary to know what d.f. means to understand this concept nor is it necessary to understand the t test.) The table or critical value for t at the .05 level of significance with 28 d.f. for a two-tailed test is 2.048. (A two-tailed test is one in which the direction of the difference (plus or minus) is not important.) This value, 2.048, was found in a t table. Such tables can be found in most statistical or research texts.

Decision

Now Mr. Philips has the necessary information to make a comparison between the two numbers. He has the computed or observed value (7.8) and the table or critical value (2.048). If the observed or computed value is less than the critical or table value, he does not reject (he accepts) the null hypothesis of no difference. He concludes that there is no significant difference between the two means. The result is probably due to chance or sampling error. If the observed or computed value is equal to or greater than the critical or table value, the null hypothesis of no difference is rejected and the conclusion is that there is a significant difference between the two means and the result is probably due to some factor other than chance or sampling error.

In this example the computed value of 7.8 is greater than the critical value of 2.048. The finding is statistically significant at the .05 level, and he rejects the null hypothesis of no difference between mean gain scores. He concludes that something other than chance or sampling error accounted for the significant finding. In this case the researcher may accept an implied or stated alternate hypothesis and conclude that the inductive treatment accounted for the difference.

Presentation of the Data

Many times results are presented in table format. See Figure 2.4. Note that the information contained in the table includes the average (mean) gain score and the standard deviation (a measure of variability) for each group. The value of the t statistic is also presented. The level of significance can be designated as $\alpha = .05$, $p < .05$, $p \leq .05$, $p > .05$, or $p \geq .05$. $\alpha = .05$ indicates that the level of significance is .05. $p < .05$ means that the level of significance is less than .05 while $p \leq .05$ means that the level of significance is less than or equal to .05. $p > .05$ indicates that the level of significance is greater than .05. $p \geq .05$ means that the finding is greater than or equal to .05. (The level of significance could be .01, .001, or some other level. If either .01 or .001 was used, that level of significance would follow the symbol.)

MEANS, STANDARD DEVIATIONS, AND t VALUE FOR TWO GROUPS

Group	Mean	Standard Deviation	N	t
Inductive	7.07	2.68	15	7.8*
Deductive	.67	1.76	15	

*Significant at the .05 level

OR

Group	N	Mean	Standard Deviation
Inductive	15	7.07	2.68
Deductive	15	.67	1.76

t = 7.8*   d.f. =28
*p $<$ .01

OR

Group	N	Mean	Standard Deviation
Inductive	15	7.07	2.68
Deductive	15	.67	1.76

t = 7.8   d.f. = 28   Significant at the .001 level

Figure 2.4. Three ways in which the
results could be presented in table form.
Note how the level of significance and the
manner of expressing it have been changed
for each example. The title above the first
table would be an appropriate title for the
other examples.

Non Significant Finding

Up to this point, an example of a finding which is significant has been explained. Very often a research result is not significant. In order to understand this, consider the following example. Below are the pretest and posttest results with the gain score for each child. See Figure 2.5. The highest possible score for either test is ten.

Inductive

Student		Pretest Score	Posttest Score	Gain Score
1.	Daniel	3	8	+5
2.	Janice	4	6	+2
3.	Jerry	5	9	+4
4.	Alice	4	3	-1
5.	Tom	6	6	0
6.	Marilyn	2	4	+2
7.	Chris	1	8	+7
8.	Linda	4	6	+2
9.	David	5	6	+1
10.	Carol	5	10	+5
11.	George	7	4	-3
12.	Melissa	6	7	+1
13.	Eugene	3	8	+5
14.	Barbara	6	10	+4
15.	Howard	3	9	+6

$\bar{X}$ gain score = 2.67

Deductive

Student		Pretest Score	Posttest Score	Gain Score
1.	Mary	0	2	+2
2.	Anthony	1	3	+2
3.	Susan	2	3	+1
4.	Paul	0	1	+1
5.	Helen	2	2	0
6.	Stephen	1	3	+2
7.	Marie	0	1	+1
8.	Mark	0	3	+3
9.	Nancy	1	4	+3
10.	Philip	4	6	+2
11.	Judy	1	5	+4
12.	John	3	1	-2
13.	Anne	2	5	+3
14.	Jack	1	3	+2
15.	Joanne	0	4	+4

$\bar{X}$ gain score = 1.87

Figure 2.5. Names, pretest, posttest, and gain scores for 30 children.

Notice that the mean gain score for the inductive group (2.67) is greater than the mean gain score (1.87) for the deductive group. Even though 2.67 is greater than 1.87, it cannot be assumed this finding is statistically significant until the appropriate statistical test is conducted and the finding is associated with a designated level of significance.

In this example, a t value of .99 is computed. The critical value for t (28 d.f.) at the .01 level of significance (two-tailed test) is 2.763. Since the observed or computed value of .99 is less than the critical or table value of 2.763, do not reject (accept) the null hypothesis and conclude that there is not a significant difference between the two means. The finding can probably be attributed to chance or sampling error.

In Figure 2.6, the results are presented in table format.

MEANS, STANDARD DEVIATIONS, AND
t VALUE FOR TWO GROUPS

Group	N	Mean	Standard Deviation
Inductive	15	2.67	2.78
Deductive	15	1.87	1.55

$t = .99$ $d.f. = 28$ n.s.

OR

Group	N	Mean	Standard Deviation
Inductive	15	2.67	2.79
Deductive	15	1.87	1.55

$t = .99$ $d.f. = 28$ $p > .05$

33

Figure 2.6. Two ways in which the results could be presented for a nonsignificant finding are presented. Note the two different ways in which a nonsignificant (n.s.) result could be expressed. The title above the first example would be an appropriate title for the second example.

Type I and Type II Errors

At times when a researcher reports his findings, he might mention that a Type I or Type II error was committed. What does this mean?

A Type I error (alpha error) is one in which the researcher rejects the null hypothesis when it should not be rejected because the null is true. He concludes that a significant difference does exist when indeed it does not exist. A Type II error (beta error) is one in which the null hypothesis is not rejected (accepted) when it is false. The researcher concludes that a difference does not exist when it does.

In this chapter many concepts were presented. A discussion pertaining to hypothesis testing and level of significance was presented. Such terms as independent and dependent variables; pre and posttests; null and alternate hypothesis; and Type I and II errors were also discussed.

EXERCISES - CHAPTER TWO

Directions: Complete the following exercises.
The answers are given at the end of the
exercises.

1. In the space provided, write "not reject" if
the null hypothesis of no difference should
not be rejected, and write "reject" if the
null hypothesis of no difference should be
rejected. The null hypothesis states that
there is no significant difference between
the mean gain achievement scores of second
grade students who are taught how to read
by using Method A when compared with other
second graders who are not taught by this
method.

_____ a. t = .65; critical value at
                  .05 level is 1.96.
_____ b. t = 3.90; critical value at
                  .05 level is 1.96.
_____ c. t = 4.20; critical value at
                  .01 level is 2.32.
_____ d. t = .35; critical value at
                  .001 level is 3.29.
_____ e. t = 3.40; critical value at
                  .001 level is 3.29.

2. Return to Problem 1, Exercises a-e. Explain
what it means when the null hypothesis is
rejected or is not rejected.

a. _____

   _____

b. _____

   _____

c. _____

   _____

d. _____

_____

e. _____

_____

3. Define the following:

a. Independent variable _____

_____

b. Dependent variable _____

_____

4. Read the following hypothesis. In each case identify the independent and dependent variables. (Fuchs, 1974)

_____ a. No significant difference
exists among the student-
_____ initiated, college super-
visor-initiated, and joint-
_____ initiated conferences with
respect to the students'
_____ attitude toward the concept
"conference."

_____

_____ b. No significant difference
exists among the student-
_____ initiated, college super-
visor-initiated, and joint-
_____ initiated conferences with
respect to the students' attitudes toward each of the
_____ following concepts: teaching
a mini lesson, being video
_____ taped, preparing the conference
agenda, discussing certain

36

_____   items (statements) during the
                    conference, and communication
_____   during the conference.

_____

_____c.   No significant difference
                    exists among the student-
                    initiated, college super-
_____   visor-initiated and joint-
                    initiated conferences with
_____   respect to the student per-
                    ceptions as to whether the
_____   conferences aided their
                    personal and/or professional
_____   growth.

_____

5. In a study by Jaus (1978) the author wanted to
    determine the effect of inservice training pro-
    grams in environmental education upon teachers'
    attitudes toward the teaching of environmental
    education.

    a. What is the independent variable? _____

        _____

    b. Why? _____

        _____

    c. What is the dependent variable? _____

        _____

    d. Why? _____

        _____

37

6. What does the .05 level of significance mean?

   _____

   _____

7. Define the following:

   a. Pretest _____

   _____

   b. Posttest _____

   _____

   c. Type I Error _____

   _____

   d. Type II Error _____

   _____

   e. Null Hypothesis _____

   _____

38

ANSWERS TO EXERCISES - CHAPTER TWO

1-2. a. .65 is less than 1.96. Do not reject
          (accept) the null hypothesis. Conclude
          that the results are not statistically
          significant and probably due to chance
          or sampling error.

      b. 3.90 is greater than 1.96. Reject the
          null hypothesis. Result is statistically
          significant and probably due to the ef-
          fect of the independent variable.

      c. 4.20 is greater than 2.32. Reject the
          null hypothesis. Result is significant
          at the .01 level of significance. Chance
          or sampling error affected the finding
          less than one per cent of the time.
          Treatment probably accounts for dif-
          ference.

      d. .35 is less than 3.29. Do not reject
          (accept) the null. Results not sig-
          nificant and probably due to chance or
          sampling error.

      e. 3.40 is greater than 3.29. Reject the
          null hypothesis. Result is significant
          at .001 level. Result probably due to
          effect of the treatment variable.

3. a. The independent variable is the manipulated
        or experimental variable.

    b. The dependent variable is the outcome
        variable.

4. a. The independent variable is the three dif-
        ferent types of conferences (student ini-
        tiated, college supervisor-initiated, and
        joint-initiated). This is the condition
        which is being manipulated. The dependent
        variable is the students' attitude toward

the concept "conference." This is the outcome variable.

b. The independent variable is the three different types of conferences. The dependent variable is the students' attitude toward the five concepts: "teaching a mini lesson," "being video taped," "preparing the conference agenda," "discussing certain items (statements) during the conference," and "communication during the conference."

c. The independent variable is the three types of conferences. The dependent variable is the students' perceptions as to whether the conferences aided their personal and/or professional growth.

5. a. The independent variable is inservice training.

    b. It is the manipulated variable.

    c. The dependent variable is attitudes of teachers.

    d. It is the outcome variable.

6. The .05 level of significance means that the probability is five times or less out of 100 that the difference is due to chance or sampling error.

7. a. A pretest is a test given to a group of subjects before the independent variable is administered.

    b. A posttest is a test given to a group of subjects after the independent variable has been administered.

    c. A Type I error means that the researcher rejects the null hypothesis when it is true.

40

d. A Type II error means that the re-
    searcher fails to reject (accepts)
    the null hypothesis when it is false.

e. The null hypothesis is the hypothesis
    of no difference.

CHAPTER THREE

UNDERSTANDING AND ANALYZING
HISTORICAL RESEARCH

Historical research is one of the major types of applied research. Although historical studies may not be as numerous as other types of research studies, such inquiry has a valid place in education.

The purpose of this chapter is to discuss what constitutes historical research and to define some of the terms appropriate to this area. After the student has read the chapter, studied the material, and completed the exercises, he should be able to:

1. Recall the purposes of historical research,

2. Define the terms primary source and secondary source,

3. Identify in a problem situation whether source material is primary, secondary, or a combination of the two,

4. Define the terms internal and external criticism, and

5. Identify in a problem situation which type of criticism is being applied.

Purposes of Historical Research

The purposes for conducting historical research are varied. This method of inquiry can be used to guide educational policymakers, to inform the curious about the past, and to challenge existing theories (Button, 1979).

A knowledge of history can be very beneficial
to today's policymakers because such knowledge
might help them to avoid errors committed in the
past. Seller (1978) investigated the reasons for
the success and failure of immigrant educators.
After she examined the evidence, she discussed
reasons why immigrant education was or was not
successful. Certainly those involved with the
education of adult immigrants such as those from
Southeast Asia would understand what worked and
did not work by reading about the history of immigrant education. Such knowledge could aid
policymakers in arriving at more sound decisions.

Lazerson (1977) also conducted a study which
can serve to guide policymakers. His research
describes a history of Catholic education. Those
involved with Catholic education might be able to
make sounder decisions if they understand what
worked and did not work and the reasons why.

Historical research can also serve to inform
about the past. Conway's (1978) essay of women's
education in the United States and Smith's (1969)
work on immigrant education give the reader information concerning the past. Such information
is useful because it helps people to understand
and learn about the past.

A study by Olneck and Lazerson (1978) also
can be helpful when learning about the past. In
this study the authors supply information concerning the school achievement of immigrant children
during the first three decades of this century.

Historians can also employ the processes of
historical research to question and/or refute
existing theories. Hogan (1978) in his work on
immigrant education challenged the theory of
Cubberley and Carlton regarding the attitudes of
immigrant parents toward American schooling.
Moore (1978) supplies an alternate hypothesis to
explain the causes of discontent between faculty

44

and students at two universities during the 1700's. She questioned the commonly held belief that the relationship between students and professors was based on feelings of consensus and community.

A historical study in the area of science education was done by Bybee (1977). In this study, he wanted to examine the past in order to support his contention (hypothesis) that science education has changed and is in the period of change regarding aims and instructional strategies. In this example, Bybee formulated a hypothesis, gathered the data, and supported his hypothesis by examining what occurred in the past.

The discovery of fossils in Ethiopia illustrates a unique type of historical research. In this study, the investigators challenged the accepted hypothesis that man's ability to walk on two legs is not related to brain development; instead the new theory states that this characteristic is linked to other factors (Dayton Daily News, 1979). In this investigation, the researchers provided evidence which was used to refute a long standing theory.

In these studies, like most historical studies, much of the material is acquired by study- ing and examining books, documents, journals, diaries, artifacts, objects, etc. Sometimes in- formation is obtained by interviewing people who have knowledge of an event.

Primary and Secondary Sources

Source material such as this can either be classified as primary or secondary. A primary source is a written or oral (sometimes taped) account of an event by someone who has witnessed the event. A secondary source is an account of an event by someone who has not witnessed the event. Because the author reports the observations of others, the testimony he receives is one, two, or

45

three times removed from the actual event.

In the Perkins study, she examined diaries of sisters who lived and worked during the Civil War. This is considered a primary source because the writers of these diaries were witnesses to these happenings.

An example of a secondary source is an account of a 1900 flood written today by a researcher who did not witness the event. Instead, the writer's narration consists of what he learned about the flood as found in newspapers, encyclopedias, or testimony received second or third hand from grandchildren and great grandchildren of the flood victims.

A person engaged in historical research attempts to have his research based upon as many primary sources as possible. The more often an account of an event is retold (rewritten), the more the researcher needs to question the veracity and accuracy of the occurrence. Stories which are told (written) and retold (rewritten) have a way of being distorted from the actual account.

Some source material cannot be classified as primary or secondary; sometimes the account of an event contains elements of both. For example, suppose a researcher found a diary of a teacher who taught in a one-room school long ago. In this diary, the teacher wrote about an epidemic which claimed the lives of many people. The teacher describes the event from his point of view (primary), and he also writes about what other teachers and others have told him (secondary).

Internal and External Criticism

In addition to being concerned with primary and secondary sources, the historical researcher needs to also subject the material to internal and external criticism. Internal criticism is a process the researcher uses to determine what the author meant by words and phrases used within a written document. External criticism is a process the investigator employs to determine the authenticity of the material.

Assume that an educational researcher uncovered a damaged book believed to be an original McGuffey Reader. Because the title page and several other pages are missing, the researcher cannot determine if the book is an original edition. When he examines the book for clues as to its authenticity, he is engaged in the process of external criticism.

Another example of the process of external criticism being applied to an object was recently related in a newspaper account of a coin found near Blue Hill Bay, Maine (Journal Herald, 1979). A noted expert on the subject of Viking coins determined that the coin is an authentic Viking coin which was minted between 1055 and 1080. This finding has tremendous implication for historians who are involved with the history of voyages to North America.

As indicated above, internal criticism is used to ascertain what the author meant by words and phrases used within a document. Many times the meaning of words changes from one generation to the next or words used many years ago are no longer used today. It is up to the historical researcher to attest to the true meaning of such words.

Imagine the job a historian will have 100 years from now when he examines documents written by people of today. Such expressions as "catch a plane," "run off 100 copies," "give me five," "down the hatch," "tie the dog loose," and "bubbler," will surely cause him extreme difficulty.

When an investigator conducts historical research, he goes through a process which is very systematic. Usually the process consists of stating a problem, reviewing the literature, describing a methodology to carry out the problem statement, arriving at results and reaching a conclusion. Sometimes he generates a hypothesis which he will use to question an existing hypothesis. The Ethiopian and Bybee investigations are examples of this.

In this chapter concepts pertaining to historical research were treated. The purposes for doing historical research as well as concepts pertaining to definitions and examples of primary and secondary source and internal and external criticism were discussed.

EXERCISES - CHAPTER THREE

Directions: Complete the following exercises.
The answers are given at the end of the
exercises.

1. In a study conducted by Clifford (1978), she
    quotes a passage from a diary written by
    Samuel Skewes in 1854. In this passage
    Skewes describes the loneliness and sorrow
    he experiences upon the death of his wife.

    a. Is this diary an example of a primary or
        secondary source? _____

        _____

    b. Why? _____

        _____

2. To determine whether or not the diary is
    authentic is an example of internal or
    external criticism? _____

    _____

3. In Conway's study (1978), she refers to a
    letter written by Benjamin Franklin. Is it
    necessary for her to determine if the letter
    is authentic?

    a. Yes   No

    b. Why? _____

        _____

49

4. While you are conducting a historical study concerning the development of the math curriculum, you locate several school board journals. These journals contain the minutes of discussions pertaining to the math curriculum carried on in the Townsbury School System from 1863 to 1910. It is your job to determine if these journals are authentic. What type of criticism do you subject these journals to?

    a. _____

    b. Why? _____

    _____

5. You also need to study the language used in the journals. You notice that through is spelled "thru" and arithmetic is referred to as "doing numbers." Adding is referred to as "doing sums." What type of criticism would you subject these words to?

    a. _____

    b. Why? _____

    _____

6. Give an example of primary and secondary source.

    _____

    _____

    _____

50

7. While conducting historical research, an investigator discovers a rare artifact from a one-room school. He determines that this artifact was made by a school supply manufacturer in 1856. What type of criticism is this?

   a. _____

   b. Why? _____

   _____

8. An account of an epidemic in 1849 appears in Mr. Doe's journal. You uncover this journal during your investigations. Is this a primary or a secondary source?

   a. _____

   b. Why? _____

   _____

ANSWERS TO EXERCISES FOR CHAPTER THREE

1a. Primary

1b. The author witnessed this event and wrote about it.

2. External

3a. Yes

3b. Open

4a. External

4b. You try to determine if the journals are actual journals written at that time.

5a. Internal.

5b. You try to determine the meaning of the terms "thru," "doing numbers," and "doing sums."

6. Open

7a. External

7b. You try to determine if the object is genuine.

8a. Primary

8b. Mr. Doe was the actual witness of the event.

CHAPTER FOUR

UNDERSTANDING AND ANALYZING
DESCRIPTIVE RESEARCH

Another major type of applied research is descriptive research. Descriptive research has as its major intent the description of what is. It consists of the following types: correlation, longitudinal, case study, ex post facto, and survey.

The purpose of this chapter is to define all of these types of research and to discuss concepts and terminology associated with descriptive research. After the student has read this chapter, studied the material, and completed the exercises, he should be able to:

1. Define and give an example of the following types of descriptive research: correlation, longitudinal, case study, ex post facto, and survey,

2. Define the following terms:

   a. Correlation coefficient,
   b. Interview,
   c. Validity, and
   d. Reliability,

3. State the numerical extremes of a correlation coefficient and interpret its meaning,

4. Recall, define, and give an example of sample, population, random sampling, stratified sampling, cluster sampling, and systematic sampling,

5. Recall and define three methods of gathering data,

6. Recall and define devices used to measure attitudes,

7. Recall and define four types of
    validity, and

8. Recall and define four types of
    reliability.

Correlation Research

One type of descriptive research is correlation research. When this method of inquiry is used, the investigation determines the degree of relationship between phenomena (variables) for the purpose of understanding relationships or predicting future outcomes. The result is expressed as a correlation coefficient which may range from -1.00 to +1.00

A positive 1.00 coefficient means that a person with a high score on one variable will have a high score on the other variable. A negative 1.00 coefficient means that a person with a high score on one variable will have a low score on the other variable. A coefficient of 0.00 means that the variables are not related.

Assume that a correlation coefficient of 0.90 was computed between two variables: motivation and achievement. This may be interpreted as indicating that as one variable increases (motivation) so does the other: a person with a high motivation score is likely to have a high achievement score. A coefficient of -0.80 means that as one variable increases, the other decreases. Therefore, a person with a high motivation score would have a low achievement score or vice versa.

In order to understand the degree of relationship between two phenomena or variables, Fuchs (1961) conducted a correlation study to assess the relationship between the rank order to teacher characteristics of an ideal teacher as expressed by seventh and ninth graders. A coefficient of 0.93 was computed for the ranking of teacher

54

qualities by seventh and ninth graders. This finding can be interpreted as indicating that both groups were similar in their ranking of the qualities of an ideal teacher.

In another correlation study, Cohen (1975) investigated the relationship between convergent and divergent thinking in selected elementary students. A coefficient of 0.52 for sixth graders indicated convergent and divergent thinking processes are related functions; a coefficient of 0.03 for seventh graders suggested that convergent and divergent thinking processes are not related.

Correlation studies can also be used as predictors of future events. With this type of investigation, the researcher tries to predict some future event based upon a present event. For example, a researcher might try to predict success in graduate school based upon graduate admission scores. A positive correlation would suggest that those with high scores would be successful in graduate school. A negative correlation would imply that the relationship between the two variables is inversely related. High scores on a test might be a poor predictor of success or vice versa.

Another example of a correlation study which was used to predict teacher survival was one conducted by Pratt (1977). In this study, the investigator studied teacher survival (future event) by examining six pre-service and two in-service variables (present event). His results suggest that of the eight variables studied, one variable (the interview) correlated significantly with teacher survival. This finding implies that the pre-service interview is a better predictor of teacher survival than such variables as sex, marital status, grade point average, type of degree, grades in curriculum subjects, and student teaching grade.

In another predictive study, Vecchio and Costin (1977) wanted to determine the relationship between successful college teaching of graduate assistants and such variables as the graduate assistant's undergraduate grade point average, scores on the Graduate Record Exam, hours of undergraduate course work in psychology, etc. Successful college teaching included student satisfaction and achievement. The authors concluded that a positive relationship existed between student achievement and the instructor's Graduate Record Exam-Advanced Score, student achievement and the number of undergraduate hours in psychology, and student satisfaction and the instructor's verbal score on the G.R.E.

Longitudinal Study

A longitudinal study is another type of descriptive research. Such a study is one in which an investigator examines and analyzes a group at more than one interval over a period of time to determine patterns and sequences of development.

Intensive longitudinal studies were completed by Gesell (1940) and Gesell and Ilg (1946). Gesell and Ilg studied growth of children age five to ten. Gesell studied the growth of children during the first five years of their lives. In both studies children were examined at specific intervals during the period of research. Results from both of these studies provide a pattern on how children develop.

Another example of a longitudinal study is the work of Piaget (Hall, 1970). Although Piaget studied only his three children, Lucienne, Laurent, and Jacqueline, over an extended period of time, he was able to construct his theory of cognitive development.

Nelson (1974) also studied cognition in young
children. In order to find out at what age certain
cognitive operations appear in young children,
Nelson examined a group of five, six, and seven
year olds during a two month period. Since Nelson
did not follow her group over a long period of
time, her study is termed a cross sectional developmental study because a cross section of
children was studied in order to determine a developmental sequence.

Case Study

A case study is another example of descriptive
research. A case study is a type of research in
which an investigator studies a unit in depth to
understand how the unit functions in its setting.
The unit can be one individual or a group such as
a class.

Suppose a teacher wishes to understand how a
disruptive student functions in his classroom. He
decides to collect information from a number of
sources such as school records, interviews with the
parents and other teachers, etc., in order to
reach an opinion concerning how this student acts
in a classroom setting. This is an example of a
case study.

Researchers could also study how a unit such
as a school or school system functions in its
setting. Such investigations are other examples
of case studies.

In an actual case study, Schramm (1974)
studied how two children with Down's Syndrome
functioned in a Montessori environment. Data from
such a study enables educators to understand how
such children interact in this type of environment.

Ex Post Facto Study

An ex post facto study is another type of descriptive research. An ex post facto study is one in which a current problem is identified. The researcher examines data in retrospect in order to determine what factors caused the problem.

An example of such a study is one in which a researcher discovers that fourth graders have vastly different group achievement scores at the end of the year. All students appear to be similar in every respect. Why, then, do some students achieve more than the others? After investigating and comparing many variables such as family background, intelligence, amount of time in school, amount of time doing homework, etc., the researcher concludes that the low achieving students completed less hours of supervised homework than did the high achieving ones. The effect, differences in achievement, was caused by the disparity in hours spent on doing supervised homework.

Another example of an ex post facto study is one conducted by Graham (1964). In this investigation Graham studied reasons why cheating among upper grade students was a problem in her school. After discovering the causes, Graham suggested remedies to solve the problem. In this study cheating was defined as the current problem, and the investigator gathered and examined the data in retrospect in order to determine the cause.

Survey Research

Survey research is another type of applied research. This kind of research can be defined as research in which one collects and analyzes opinions or attitudes of a group toward a topic.

An example of a survey study is one conducted by Luce and Johnson (1978). In this investigation, the authors asked respondents to rate journals in the areas of education and psychology. A

58

questionnaire was used to gather the opinions of
the respondents.

A questionnaire was employed in a survey study
by Pietras and Lamb (1978). Respondents were asked
to express their attitudes toward non-standard
black dialects.

Sample and Population

In many studies, descriptive as well as experimental, the researcher wishes to generalize
his results from a sample to a population. A
population is a group which has one or more traits
in common and is selected for study; a sample is
a part of the population which is chosen for analysis.

A teacher wants to study the effectiveness of
a teaching method on seventh graders. In his
school, 250 seventh graders are enrolled. He is
able to describe this population in terms of intelligence, achievement, family background, etc.
Since it is not possible for him to use all of the
students, he decides to select by a scientific
process a group of 30 students who will participate.
If he has employed an acceptable method of selecting his sample, he can generalize his results to
the whole class of 250 students. These results
cannot be generalized to other schools because they
were not members of the population. If a researcher
defines his population as all seventh grades in his
city and selects a representative sample from that
population, then he can generalize the results to
that group.

Consider another example. Suppose a researcher wanted to find out the opinion of elementary
teachers toward the concept of team teaching. He
defines as his population all certified elementary
teachers (grades one through six) in the United
States. Obviously, it would be too expensive and
too impractical for him to survey all the teachers.

59

He needs to select a small proportion of people (a sample) which will represent the population.

Sampling Techniques

Selecting a small group to represent a population can be done by employing one of four sampling techniques. These are random, stratified random, systematic, or cluster sampling.

Random Sample

A random sample means that each individual who forms the sample is picked in such a fashion that each individual has an equal chance of being selected. To ensure that each member of the population has an equal chance of being selected, a table of random numbers is often used as a means of selecting the sample.

Assume that a researcher has defined his population as all of the 10,000 teachers who are employed by the city of Markus. He wishes to survey them to find out their opinion concerning grading procedures. Since he cannot survey all 10,000, he decides to select a sample of 1000.

By using a table of random numbers the researcher is able to select his sample so that each individual in the population has an equal chance of being selected and each choice is independent of any other selection.

Stratified Random Sample

Another way to select a sample is to employ the process of stratified random sampling. When this method is used, the population is divided into parts. From each part members are selected in the same proportion as they appear in the population.

In the example above, the researcher wishes to have proportionate representation from all categories of teachers. He realizes that from his population of 10,000 teachers, 65 per cent or 6500 teachers teach at the elementary level, 20 per cent (2000) teach at the junior high level, and 15 per cent (1500) teach at the senior high level. If a random sample is drawn, he might by pure chance select a sample of 80 per cent elementary teachers, 15 per cent junior high teachers, and 5 per cent senior high teachers. This percentage of teachers in each category is not in proportion to the population. By employing the stratified random sample procedure, the researcher would ensure the 65 per cent of this sample is comprised of elementary teachers, 20 per cent junior high, and 15 per cent senior high.

Systematic Sample

A systematic sample is one in which members are selected in a systematic fashion. Assume the names of the 10,000 teachers were arranged in alphabetical order, and the researcher wishes to select a sample of 1000. By selecting every tenth name on the list, the researcher would eventually end up with his sample. All the names were selected in a systematic manner.

Cluster Sample

A cluster sample is one in which groups are chosen to form the sample. Assume that a researcher defines as his population all 8000 first grade classrooms in the state of Ohio. Because it is impractical for the researcher to randomly select individual classes to form his sample, he elects to select groups or clusters. In this example the researcher randomly selects ten counties from all the counties in the state. From each county the researcher randomly selects five schools. From each school he randomly selects one first grade. His final sample consists of those first grade classrooms.

Data Collection

Data can be collected in a number of ways: observation, interviews, and questionnaires.

Observation

Observation of behavior is a method sometimes employed to collect data. The investigator defines what behavior he wishes to observe, decides how to record what he has observed, and provides some indication that his observations are consistent.

For example, suppose a researcher wishes to observe what verbal expressions teachers use when praising children. The researcher needs to decide which expressions constitute praise. Such expressions as "good," "fine," "all right," etc., might be selected. Next, the researcher decides to count the number of times each expression is used during a given period of time. Finally, to ensure that his observations of behavior are accurate and consistent, he needs to demonstrate inter-observer reliability. Usually this is accomplished by having one or more observers record the behaviors at the same time as the investigator. The results are then correlated with one another. A high correlation indicates a high degree of consistency.

Interviews

Interviews are also used to collect data. Sometimes, the interviewer asks an interviewee a series of predetermined questions. Such an interview is highly structured. At other times an interviewer might ask the interviewee a set of open ended questions. Such a procedure allows for more penetrating questions on the part of a skilled interviewer.

Questionnaires

Questionnaires are also used to collect data

in the form of opinions or attitudes. Two common
types of devices are the Likert scale (1932) and
the semantic differential (Osgood, Luci and Tannenbaum, 1957). The Likert scale measures a person's
attitude toward a subject by asking him to respond
to questions by selecting from one of three, four,
or five responses. For example, often times the
responses "strongly approve", "approve", "undecided",
"disapprove", or "strongly disapprove" are used.
The semantic differential consists of a concept to
be measured, a series of bipolar adjectives, and
undefined scale positions.

Sometimes a researcher will report that his
questionnaire or other paper and pencil measuring
instrument (example, commercially prepared tests)
is valid and/or reliable.[1] What is meant by these
terms?

Validity

Validity refers to the characteristic of
stating that the questionnaire measures what it
claims to measure. A questionnaire used to gather
opinions of teachers toward the usefulness of team
teaching is valid if it can be shown that it does
measure such opinions.

To indicate that an instrument is valid, a
researcher can provide evidence to substantiate
this fact. He can claim his device is valid by
one of four ways: content, predictive, concurrent,
and construct.

Content validity means that the instrument is
valid because the researcher has placed items on
the test or questionnaire based upon a systematic

---

[1]For a detailed discussion of validity and
reliability, see Thorndike and Hagen (1969) or
Anastasi (1976).

and thorough examination of an area. A researcher who wishes to construct an instrument to measure what respondents feel the characteristics of an ideal teacher are could prove that his instrument is valid because only those characteristics mentioned most frequently in the literature are included.

Predictive validity is defined as that type of validity which will attempt to measure how someone will do in a future setting. A test of mechanical aptitude has a high predictive value if it can predict rather accurately which students will and will not become successful auto mechanics.

Concurrent validity is another type of validity. Concurrent validity is defined as the degree to which scores on one test are related to scores on another similar test which has been determined to be valid. If, for example, a researcher developed an achievement test used to determine achievement of students in science, he would administer his test and an established science achievement test and compute a correlation coefficient between the two sets of scores.

Construct validity is another type of validity. Construct validity is defined as how well a test measures a theoretical construct. A construct is usually a phenomenon which is not observable. Intelligence, attitudes, and feelings are examples of such phenomenon.

Reliability

In addition to a test or questionnaire being valid, it should also be reliable. The reliability of a test refers to its ability to measure consistently the same concept from one administration of the test to another. The reliability of a test can be determined in one of four ways: test-retest, equivalent forms, split half, and rationale equivalence.

Test-retest reliability means that scores on the administration of a test are correlated with scores on subsequent administrations of the test. Because the same test needs to be given to the same group a second time, this factor can be a disadvantage to a researcher who cannot retest the same group a second time.

Equivalent form reliability is computed by correlating a test score with test scores of an equivalent or parallel test.

Split half reliability is another way to determine reliability. It is determined by dividing the test into two sections (odd problems and even problems, for example) and computing a correlation coefficient between the halves.

Rationale equivalence reliability can also be used to determine reliability. It is computed by using Kuder-Richardson formulas 20 or 21. (Kuder and Richardson, 1937)

Concepts pertaining to descriptive research were discussed in this chapter. The five types of descriptive research included correlation, longitudinal, case study, ex post facto, and survey. Also discussed were sampling procedures, methods of gathering data, and test validity and reliability.

Directions: Complete the following exercises.
The answers are given at the end of the
exercises.

1.   Define the following types of research and
      give an example of each:

      a-b. Correlation _____

      _____

      _____

      c-d. Longitudinal _____

      _____

      _____

      e-f. Case study _____

      _____

      _____

      g-h. Ex post facto _____

      _____

      _____

      i-j. Survey _____

      _____

      _____

2.   Define correlation coefficient _____

      _____

3. What is the highest possible correlation coefficient that could exist between two variables?

_____

4. Assume a researcher computed a correlation coefficient of −.80 between school grades and intelligence of students. How can this finding be interpreted?

_____

_____

5. McTeer and Blanton (1975) administered an opinionnaire to students. The reliability coefficient of the instrument was reported to be +.92.

   a. Is this coefficient acceptable? _____

   b. Why or why not? _____

_____

6. In a study by Alvord and Brittingham (1974) the population was defined as fourth grade students in Iowa. In order to ensure that the sample (1105 students) would be proportionally representative of urban, suburban, and rural schools, what sampling technique do you think the researcher used?

_____

7. Define the term random sampling. _____

_____

_____

8. From an alphabetical list of 10,000 names, every 10th name is selected to receive a questionnaire through the mail. What kind of sampling technique is this?

_____

9. List and define the three methods used to gather data.

a-b. _____

_____

c-d. _____

_____

e-f. _____

_____

10. What two devices could be used to measure attitudes?

a. _____

b. _____

11. Define validity. _____

_____

12. Define reliability. _____

_____

13. Fuchs (1961) constructed a questionnaire to measure attitudes of students toward qualities of an ideal teacher. Items presented on the questionnaire were obtained from qualities mentioned in the literature. What types of validity can the researcher claim?

_____

Why? _____

_____

14. If a researcher correlates future performances with a group's scores on a written test, what type of validity is this?

_____

15. Epstein and McPartland (1976) used the Kuder-Richardson formula number 20 to obtain a reliability coefficient for an instrument they developed. What type of reliability coefficient is this?

_____

16. Moos (1978) used the test-retest method of determining reliability of an instrument. What does this mean?

_____

_____

17. Nevill, Ware, and Smith (1978) used the test-retest method to determine a reliability coefficient of a questionnaire. They retested their subjects after one week and reported a coefficient of +.67.

a. Is this coefficient acceptable? _____

b. Why or why not? _____

_____

c. If a reliability coefficient of +.67 was
    reported after six weeks, would this be
    acceptable? _____

d. Why or why not? _____

_____

ANSWERS TO THE EXERCISES FOR CHAPTER FOUR

1a. A correlation study is one in which a relationship between variables is examined.

1b. Open

1c. A longitudinal study is one in which an investigator examines and analyzes a group over
a period of time to determine patterns and
sequences of development.

1d. Open

1e. A case study is one in which a person studies
a unit in depth to understand how the unit
functions in its setting.

1f. Open

1g. An ex post facto study is one in which a person
identifies a problem and then searches for its
cause.

1h. Open

1i. A survey study is one in which a person collects
and analyzes attitudes or opinions.

1j. Open

2. A correlation coefficient states the degree of
relationship between variables.

3. The highest possible correlation is +1.00.

4. A negative .80 correlation means that as one
variable increased, the other decreased.

5a. Yes

5b. This relationship is very high.

6. Stratified random sample

7. A random sample is one in which a researcher selects his sample in such a fashion that each individual has an equal chance of being selected.

8. Systematic sample

9a. Observation

9b. A unit of behavior is observed.

9c. Interview

9d. A technique in which the researcher asks people answers to questions.

9e. Questionnaire

9f. A paper and pencil device used to gather attitudes or opinions.

10a. Osgood's semantic differential

10b. Likert scale

11. Validity is the ability of the test to measure what it claims to measure.

12. Reliability is the ability of the test to measure consistently.

13a. Content

13b. The items were placed on the opinionnaire because they occurred often in the literature.

14. Predictive

15. Rationale equivalence

16. After a period of time, the same test is given. Scores from the first test are cor- related with scores from the second test.

17a. Open

17b. Open

17c. Open

17d. Open

CHAPTER FIVE

UNDERSTANDING AND ANALYZING
EXPERIMENTAL RESEARCH

Experimental research is another type of applied research. This type of research permits the investigator to study cause and effect relationships. In order to understand and analyze this type of research, the consumer of educational research should be knowledgeable about the terms and methods associated with experimental research.

The purpose of this chapter is to discuss and explain concepts related to experimental research. After the student has read this chapter, studied the material, and completed the exercises, he should be able to:

1. Define the following terms:

    a. Research design,
    b. Internal and external validity,
    c. Extraneous variable,
    d. Classical and factorial designs,
    e. Main effects,
    f. Interaction,
    g. The symbols - E, R, C, X, T_1, T_2 and
    h. The factors which jeopardize internal and external validity.

2. Give an example of each of the following:

    a. Classical and factorial designs,
    b. Main effects,
    c. Interaction, and
    d. Extraneous variable.

3. Analyze in an experimental design the factors which affect the internal and external validity of the design.

4. Recall Stanley and Campbell's four
    categories of experimental design,

5. Identify in diagram form different types
    of classical designs and a 2 x 2 factorial
    design, and

6. State the appropriate design to use when
    presented with a research problem.

What is a research design? A research design
is simply a preconceived plan a researcher employs
which enables him to conduct his research in a
systematic fashion. The design mentioned in
Chapter Two is an example of a preconceived plan
which consisted of two groups of students. Each
group was pretested, subjected to a treatment,
and posttested.

Internal and External Validity

Many designs are available to the researcher.
If an established design does not fit the investigator's plan, he can modify an existing one
or create a new one. No matter what design a
researcher selects, he must be aware of factors
which could affect the validity of a design. The
two major sources of validity are internal and
external (Campbell and Stanley, 1966). Internal
validity asks the question whether or not the
manipulation of the independent variable caused a
difference in the dependent variable. The researcher wants to be able to claim that his
treatment variable and not one or more extraneous
variables[1] made a difference. External validity

------

[1]An extraneous variable is one which is not
controlled. Since it is not controlled, it could
influence the outcome of the experiment by sug-
gesting to the researcher that these variables and
not the manipulation of the treatment variables
produced the result.

is used to determine to which setting outside the experimental setting a researcher can generalize his results.

Factors Affecting Internal Validity

A number of extraneous variables can threaten the internal validity of an experiment because the influence of these variables could be mistaken for the effect of the treatment. These variables include the effect of history, effect of maturation, influence of pretest, change in instrumentation, differential selection of participants, statistical regression and experimental mortality.[2]

Effect of History

The effect of history can be defined as those uncontrolled events which occur between the administration of the pretest and posttest. Suppose a teacher wishes to determine how effective an individualized approach to teaching about traffic safety is upon safety achievement of his thirty students. He pretests his students, uses this approach for six weeks, and posttests his students.

The teacher computes the average pretest score to be 35%. During the fourth and fifth weeks of the experiment, numerous accidents occur in the area. Both the printed and electronic news media cover the accounts of the accidents in great detail. After the experiment, the class is post-tested. The average score for the class is 75%. The teacher concludes that the experiment is a success because the treatment was successful as reflected by the higher average posttest score.

---

[2]The discussion of internal validity has been based upon the work of Campbell and Stanley (1966).

The question must be asked whether the improved performance on the posttest was due to the method of teaching or due to the fact that the 30 students could have been sensitized to traffic safety because of the news coverage of the accidents. This extraneous variable could be mistaken for the effect of the planned independent variable.

Effect of Maturation

The effect of maturation is another factor which can threaten internal validity. Because participants in experiments mature, these effects can be mistaken for treatment effects. Stephen, a preschooler, has difficulty making certain speech sounds. A speech therapist tests his sounds (pretest) to determine his level of speech. Because his speech pattern deviates from the norm for children his age, speech therapy is suggested.

For two years, Stephen attends speech classes two times a week. At the end of the two year period, he is again tested by the speech therapist who determines that his speech is now normal for children his age. During the two years, Stephen's psychomotor skills, listening skills, physical abilities, etc., probably improved because he matured. Was Stephen's improvement due to the speech therapy or was it due to the fact that Stephen matured?

Influence of Pretest

Pretesting effects can also jeopardize internal validity. This occurs because the pretest serves as a learning experience, and those who are pretested become "test wise" because the questions on the pretest might alert them to posttest questions. Since their posttest scores could be higher because they become "test wise" by taking the pretest, this extraneous variable could be mistaken for the effect of the treatment. To eliminate this factor use an experimental design in which

78

the subjects are not pretested or use a different form for the pretest and posttest.

Change in Instrumentation

Change in instrumentation is another element which could threaten internal validity. Assume the pretest is a fifty item objective test which is difficult. The posttest is also a fifty item objective test, but it is very easy, thus reflecting higher posttest scores. Are the results due to the method or due to the differences in the difficulty of the tests?

Another example of the change of instrumentation is the use of different raters. For example, a pretest is an essay test graded by one set of people. The essay type posttest is scored by a different group. Are the results due to the effect of the method or due to the different grading styles of the raters?

Statistical Regression

Statistical regression is another phenomenon which may affect the internal validity of a design. It can occur when students are selected to participate in a study on the basis of extremely high or low scores. Upon retesting, those who had low pretest scores may score higher on the posttest and those who had high pretest scores may score lower on the posttest.

Assume that a researcher wants to discover if his method of teaching reading will succeed with very poor readers. He selects 50 students with the lowest reading ability to participate in the experiment. To serve as a comparison group he selects 50 bright students. All the students are given a pretest. At the conclusion of the study he posttests all the students. When the researcher examines his data, he discovers that the mean score for the low ability students is higher than their mean pretest score. He also discovers that the

79

posttest scores for the comparison group are lower than their pretest scores. He concludes that his method produced the result instead of realizing that the phenomenon of statistical regression could have occurred.

Differential Selection of Participants

Differential selection of participants is another factor which could affect internal validity. Assume a teacher wishes to determine how effective the use of praise is on the retention of arithmetic facts. She divides the class into two equal groups of 15 students. Group A receives praise on specific occasions while Group B does not receive any praise. At the end of the six week experiment, both groups are posttested. Group A's average on the posttest is higher than Group B's. The teacher concludes the method was responsible for the better results.

The effects of selection of the participants could have caused the higher achievement in Group A. It is entirely possible that the students in Group A knew the arithmetic facts better than the pupils in Group B, thus the results are not due to the method.

Another example of how the differential selection of subjects can be mistaken for the treatment effect is the use of volunteers and non-volunteers. Assume that out of a group of 50 students, 25 volunteered to participate in an experiment and 25 did not. Posttest scores for the group which volunteered are much higher than the posttest scores for the non-volunteer group. The teacher concludes that the method was effective whereas the superior posttest scores could be due to the fact that the children were intrinsically motivated because they volunteered to participate.

Experimental Mortality

Another factor which can affect internal validity is experimental mortality. Suppose that after an experiment begins, several of the students with the lowest pretest scores leave the school because of moving out of the district or some other legitimate reason. Left in the experiment are those who scored high on the pretest. The post-test mean is greater than the pretest mean. The teacher might incorrectly conclude that the experiment was a success. The scores of the low achieving students who dropped out of the study could have had an effect on the posttest mean.

These seven factors, then, can have an effect upon the internal validity of an experiment. A consumer of educational research needs to be aware of these as well as the factors which can jeopardize external validity when he reads the literature.

Factors Affecting External Validity

If a researcher wishes to be able to generalize his findings beyond his experimental setting, he needs to be concerned with the factors which might affect the external validity of his study. Factors which could jeopardize external validity are the confounding effects produced by pretesting, the interaction effect of selection and treatment, confounding effect of experimental procedures, and the interference caused by multiple treatments.[3]

Confounding Effect of Pretesting

One source of external validity is the confounding effect of pretesting. When students take a pretest and then undergo the treatment, the pretest could sensitize the students to what the

---

[3]The discussion of external validity is based upon Campbell and Stanley (1966). Also see Bracht and Glass (1968).

treatment is, therefore, increased or decreased posttest scores could be the result of this sensitization and not the effects of the treatment.

Suppose 100 eighth grade students participate in an experiment in which the treatment is a method of instilling favorable attitudes toward proper nutrition. The pretest is given, and the items in the pretest alert the students to what they will be taught. After the treatment has been applied and the posttest administered, an increase or decrease in the pretest and posttest comparison might not be due to the treatment; it might be due to the fact that the pretest sensitized or alerted the students to what the experiment was about. In this case the results are generalizable only to those groups in the population which were pretested. Usually this includes those subjects in the experimental and control groups and not others in the population.

Interaction Effect of Selection and Treatment

Another source of external validity is the interaction effects of selection and treatment. This factor means that an experimenter needs to be careful when he generalizes his findings from a sample to a population.

Assume that the independent variable is the teaching of science by using an individualized approach. In a school, a researcher randomly selects 30 of the 100 fifth grade students to participate. The results can be generalized to the 100 students in the study, and not to other fifth grade classes in the district or state. If he conducts this experiment with the fifth grades in the district and randomly selects a sample from this population, he can generalize the results to that population; he cannot generalize the results to other districts.

Confounding Effects of Experimental Procedures

The confounding effects of the experimental arrangements can also jeopardize external validity. If the subjects of an experiment are aware that they are participating in an experiment, they may alter their performance because of this.

For example, three classrooms are designated as the experimental classrooms. During the experiment, observers come into the experimental classroom to check on the pupils' progress or special equipment such as closed circuit television which is employed. These conditions could alert the class to the fact that something unusual is happening. This kind of special attention could affect the results of the experiment because the participants might act differently under these conditions. The experimenter cannot generalize his results to other situations where these conditions were not present.

Interference Caused by Multiple Treatments

Multiple treatment interference is another factor which could have an effect on external validity. When the subjects of an experiment are exposed to many treatments, it is difficult to block out the effects of the other treatments. If this is the case, the results may be generalized to those who have experienced the same sequences of treatments. For example, the researcher decides to use three forms of praise to reward students. The three treatments are verbal praise, written praise, and a combination of the two.

Verbal praise is administered and then a posttest is given. Several days later, this is followed by the use of written praise and a posttest. Several days later, this in turn is followed by the combination of verbal and written praise and the posttest. Before administering the second treatment, the effects of the first treatment need

to be erased. Similarly, before beginning the
third treatment, the effects of the first and
second treatments need to be eliminated. If they
are not, the researcher cannot determine which
treatment was more effective, nor can he generalize results to other situations unless the sequence
is presented in the same way.

These then, are the factors which can jeopardize
external validity.

When the consumer of educational research reads
the literature, he needs to be aware of the factors
which could jeopardize the validity of the study.
In order to help the consumer understand this, he
needs to understand experimental design as well
as what design was used. To determine what design
was used, it is probably necessary for him to draw
an illustration of it and then determine which
sources of validity are controlled, not controlled,
or have no bearing on the design.

Classical Designs

Experimental designs have been classified in
a number of ways. Cook (1965) divided experimental
designs into two categories: equivalent group
design and factorial design. An equivalent group
design is one in which one independent variable
is manipulated; with a factorial design, more
than one independent variable is manipulated.

Wise, Nordberg, and Reitz (1967) classified
experimental design as functional and factorial.
According to these authors, a functional design
is one in which the experimenter can manipulate
the independent variable at will; a factorial
design is one in which the researcher cannot
manipulate the treatment variable at will.

Probably the most complete categorization of
designs has been advanced by Campbell and Stanley

84

(1966). In their text they present 16 designs
classified into four categories: pre-experimental,
true experimental, quasi experimental, and correlational ex post facto.

For the purpose of this discussion, designs
will be classified as either classical or
factorial. A classical design is one in which
the researcher manipulates only one independent
variable. He is able to vary that variable and
study its effects on the dependent variable. A
factorial design is one in which the effects of
two or more independent variables, each with two
or more levels, on a dependent variable are studied.

Design One[4]

Assume that 30 students were taught spelling

---

[4]The works of Campbell and Stanley (1966),
Best (1977), Van Dalen (1979), Solomon (1949) and
others have had an influence on the author's con-
ception of designs.

Each design has been named using the following
format: the number of groups, identification of
the groups - E for experimental and C for control,
the type of group - randomized or non randomized,
and the testing arrangements - pretest and/or
posttest.

The following symbols are used: E = experimental group, C = control group, R = random
assignment to a group, X = application of the
independent variable, T_1 = pretest observation,
and T_2 = posttest observation.

The consumer of educational research should
be aware of the fact that different writers
identify the same design by different names and
use different symbols. To understand completely
what an author is discussing, the consumer must
know the terminology used by that author.

by listening to a series of lessons presented on
a tape. After the six week experiment has ended,
the teacher gives the students a posttest. The
average posttest score is 85% out of 100%. The
teacher is very satisfied with the results and
feels that this method produced the better results.
Perhaps this feeling is warranted, but the design
should be subjected to factors which affect its
internal and external validity before a final
conclusion is reached.

In determining which factors threaten the
validity of the above experiment it is helpful if
a diagram of the design is drawn. See Figure 5.1
for an illustration of this design.

(E)   X T_2

Figure 5.1. One group, (E), non randomized,
posttest only design.

The factors which affect the design's validity are the effect of history, effect of maturation, differential selection of participants, and
experimental mortality.

The effect of history is not controlled because an intervening event could cause the students
to learn to spell better. The effect of maturation
is not controlled because as the children mature,
they might learn to spell better, thus, the improved achievement is not the result of the method.
Differential selection of participants is not
controlled because it is very possible that the
students were good spellers to begin with, and
thus, this factor could account for improved performance and not the treatment. Experimental
mortality is not controlled. If the poor spellers
drop out of the experiment leaving only the average
and good spellers, this could account for a high
performance on the posttest.

Several sources of internal validity are not

86

affected by this design. These include the influence of pretesting, change in instrumentation, and
statistical regression. Since a pretest is not
administered, the effects of pretesting, instrumentation, and statistical regression are not
sources of concern.

With respect to external validity, the interaction effects of selection and treatment are not
controlled. Because the students who participated
in this experiment have not been randomly assigned
to the treatment group, the researcher cannot
generalize his findings to a population. The
other three sources of external validity are not
a concern in this design because a pretest is not
given, (confounding effects of pretesting), only
one group is used (confounding effects of experimental procedures), and multiple treatments are
not applied.

Because few sources of internal and external
validity are not controlled, this design is a very
weak one. It is presented to illustrate that one
cannot claim success with a teaching method when
this design is applied. For example, in many
school situations, teachers teach and then test.
Are the grades received the result of their teaching or the results of such extraneous variables as
history, maturation, mortality, etc.?

Design Two

Because this design is a weak one, the teacher
decides to pretest the students in order to lessen
the factors which threaten internal validity. The
students score 35% on the pretest, receive the
treatment for six weeks, and are posttested. The
average score for the posttest is 90%, a mean gain
of 55%. See Figure 5.2 for an illustration of
this design.

$$(E) \qquad T_1 \qquad X \qquad T_2$$

Figure 5.2. One group, (E), non randomized,
pretest-posttest design.

Because of the large increase in mean gain score, the teacher claims the gain resulted from the method used. If he checks to determine which factors threaten the internal and external validity of this design, he soon discovers that this design contains many weaknesses.

The sources of internal validity which pose a threat include the effect of history, the effect of maturation, pretesting influences, and change in instrumentation. Because only one group is used, the effects of history and maturation are not controlled. Since a pretest is given, it could serve as a learning device by alerting the students to possible posttest questions. Instrumentation is not controlled. If the posttest is less challenging than the pretest, this effect and not the treatment could account for any improved scores.

The two sources of internal validity which are controlled are differential selection of participants and experimental mortality. Differential selection of participants is controlled because a group which is composed of good spellers will be pretested before the experiment began; thus the entering behavior is compared to the posttest performance. The effects of mortality are controlled since students who drop out of the experiment will not be posttested; therefore, their pretest scores are not used to compute a pretest average.

Statistical regression is a source of concern in this design. Assume poor spellers are selected to participate because they are poor spellers, and as a group, they do poorly on the pretest. They will most likely do better on the posttest because of statistical regression. This phenomenon could be interpreted incorrectly as producing the gain in achievement.

Two sources of external validity which are not controlled are confounding effects of pretesting and the interaction effects of selection and treatment. The use of the pretest could sensitize the students to what will happen during the experiment. Because the group has not been selected on a random basis, the experimenter cannot generalize his results to a population, thus the interaction effect of selection and treatment is not controlled.

The confounding effect of experimental procedure is a source of concern with this design. If observers are used to monitor the teacher's performance or to check on the progress of the pupils, the students might behave differently when outside observers have entered the classroom.

Multiple treatment interference is not a source of concern in this design. Only one treatment is administered.

Design Three

So far, the discussion has included two designs in which only one group is used. Suppose the teacher adds a control group and still retains an experimental group. A control group is a group which is used to make a comparison to the experimental group. Members of this group do not receive the experimental treatment. See Figure 5.3 for an illustration of this design.

(E)	T_1	X	T_2
(C)	T_1		T_2

Figure 5.3. Two groups, (E/C), non randomized, pretest-posttest design.

Assume the experimental group (E) receives the treatment. The treatment consists of teaching reading by using the language experience approach. Their average pretest score is 20%; their average posttest score is 90%, a gain of 70%. The control group (C) is pretested and posttested, but they do not receive any treatment. Their average pretest

89

score is 50%; their average posttest score is also 90%, a gain of 40%. After applying the appropriate statistical test and comparing this value to a designated level of significance, the null hypothesis is rejected, and the teacher concludes that the method produced the difference. Is this conclusion valid? Again, this design needs to be subjected to the sources of internal validity to determine if these factors could have accounted for the significant finding.

Because a control group is used, the effect of history, maturation, pretesting influences, and change in instrumentation are controlled. Both groups will probably experience the same historical events, mature at the same rate, be affected the same way by taking a pretest, and be similarly influenced by instrumentation. Experimental mortality is also controlled because the experimenter can determine who dropped out of the experiment. If all the low scoring pupils drop out of the experimental group, the investigator needs to be aware of this when he compares the groups' achievement.

Statistical regression and differential selection of participants are sources of concern. If the experimental group is composed of all the low ability students who score poorly on the pretest and the control group consists of all the intelligent students who score high on the pretest, the slow group might score higher on the posttest and the fast group might score lower on the posttest because of this pehnomenon. Differential selection of participants could also be a source of concern if by some quirk all of the better readers composed the experimental group and the poor readers were in the control group, or if volunteers comprised the experimental group and non-volunteers comprised the control group.

With respect to external validity, the confounding effects of pretesting are not controlled. The pretest could sensitize the experimental group to the treatment. Thus, the results can only be generalized to others in the population who have been pretested.

Interaction effects of selection and treatment are a source of concern. Because the groups have not been assigned on a random basis, the investigator cannot generalize his findings. The confounding effects of experimental procedures are also a source of concern. If the students in the experimental group know they are participating in an experiment, this could have an effect upon their posttest scores. The results cannot be generalized to other groups who were not exposed to the same procedures.

Multiple treatment interference is not a cause for concern in this design. Only one treatment is used.

Design Four

The teacher used Design Three because he had to use intact classrooms; he could not select the students in a random manner. Suppose the principal allows the teacher to select members for each group by using the process of randomization.[4] The experimental group's treatment consists of learning how to read by using a language experience approach. The control group does not recieve this treatment. In Figure 5.4 is illustrated a design in which members of each group have been assigned on a random basis. (Some researchers will not only assign subjects on a random basis, they will also assign the treatment on a random basis.)

---

[4]Both Stanley (1966) and Yates (1964) credit Sir Ronald A. Fischer with introducing the principle of randomization. See the bibliography for Fischer's publications.

$$R \quad (E) \quad T_1 \quad X \quad T_2$$

$$R \quad (C) \quad T_1 \quad \quad T_2$$

Figure 5.4. Two groups, (E/C), randomized, pretest-posttest design.

After the experiment, the teacher computes the results and rejects the null hypothesis. He concludes that the finding is significant. Did the experimental variable make a difference? In order to answer this question, the design must be subjected to the factors which affect internal validity.

The effect of history, maturation, pretesting influences, and change in instrumentation are controlled for the same reasons as explained for Design Three. Because the students are assigned to groups on a random basis, statistical regression, differential selection of participants, and experimental mortality are also controlled.

With respect to external validity, the confounding effect of pretesting is not controlled. Students in the experimental group could become sensitized to the treatment because of taking the pretest.

The interaction effects of selection and treatment and confounding effects of experimental procedure are of concern. If the sampling procedure is conducted in a scientific way, then the interaction effect of selection and treatment is taken care of. The confounding effects of experimental procedure can be of concern if the students in the experimental group are visited by observers, etc., and those in the control group are not visited.

The multiple treatment interference is not a source of external validity for this design. Only one treatment is administered.

Design Five

The teacher is satisfied that Design Four controlled the factors which affect internal validity thus indicating that the experimental treatment accounted for any significant finding. Now the teacher would like to be able to control as many factors as possible which affect external validity because he is interested in generalizing his results.

The teacher replicated the reading experiment mentioned above, but he does not pretest either group. See Figure 5.5 for a diagram of this design.

R   (E)   X T_2

R   (C) T_2

Figure 5.5. Two groups, (E/C), randomized, posttest only.

Which sources of internal validity threaten this design? None, because a control group and randomization are used. The use of randomization is one procedure a researcher can use to equate groups. (For other procedures which can be used to equate groups see Best, 1977).

Of the four factors which affect the design's external validity, one is controlled.

The confounding effects of pretesting are controlled because a pretest is not given. Both the interaction effects of selection and treatment and the confounding effects of experimental procedure are of concern in this design for the same reasons as stated for Design Four. The multiple treatment interference is of no concern with the design.

Up to this point the discussion has treated designs in which one or two groups have been used.

93

Are designs available in which more than two groups are used?

Design Six

The teacher decides to combine Designs Four and Five in order to study the treatment when applied under different conditions. This combination results in a design attributed to Solomon (1949) which consists of four groups. See Figure 5.6 for an illustration of this design.

R	(E)	T_1	X	T_2
R	(C)	T_1		T_2
R	(E)		X	T_2
R	(C)			T_2

Figure 5.6. Solomon Four, (E/C/E/C), randomized, 2 pretests - 4 posttests.

Note that two groups are pretested and two groups are not. Also note that the treatment is administered to two groups.

The factors affecting the sources of internal and external validity are the same as those explained in Design Five. If this is the case, why use this design? The use of this design permits the teacher to study multiple comparisons.

Design Seven

Recall that the independent variable associated with Design Four was the teaching of reading by using the language experience approach. A control group was also employed.

Now the teacher wishes to experiment with two approaches to the teaching of reading: the basal approach and the language experience approach. In Figure 5.7 this design is illustrated.

R   (E)   Level 1 T_1 X T_2
           Basal Approach

R   (E)   Level 2 T_1 X T_2
           Language Exper-
           ience Approach

Figure 5.7. Two groups, (E/E), randomized, pretest-posttest design.

Note that a control group is not used. Also note that the independent variable, a method of teaching reading, has two levels - the basal approach and the language experience approach.

With this design, all sources of internal validity are held in check.

With respect to the factors which jeopardize external validity, the confounding effects of pretesting are not controlled because a pretest is used. The interaction effects of selection and treatment are a source of concern if the sampling procedures are not valid. The confounding effects of experimental procedure are controlled. Since both groups are exposed to a treatment, each treatment will probably need to be monitored, thus, observers will be used in each group. The multiple treatment interference is not of concern.

Design Eight

If an investigator wishes to determine which of three approaches to the teaching of reading is the best, he now has an independent variable with three levels. See Figure 5.8.

95

R	(E)	Level 1 Basal Approach	T_1	X	T_2
R	(E)	Level 2 Language Experience Approach	T_1	X	T_2
R	(E)	Level 3 Phonetic Approach	T_1	X	T_2

Figure 5.8. Three groups, (E/E/E), randomized, pretest-posttest design.

All sources of internal validity are controlled. The factors which affect the external validity are the same as those discussed for Design Seven.

Eight classical designs have been presented. Factors which affect validity for each of these designs have also been discussed.

These are not the only classical designs available. An investigator could combine designs or devise one of his own. No matter which design is used, the researcher as well as the consumer of research should be aware of the sources of validity.

Factorial Designs

The second classification of design is factorial design. This design was operationalized by Fischer in Design of Experiments. (Yates, 1964)

The use of a factorial design allows the experimenter to test two or more independent variables each with two or more levels.

Assume a researcher wishes to determine the effectiveness of teaching science in two different ways, expository and discovery, and type of classroom organization, structured and nonstructured, on achievement. This experiment is diagrammed in Figure 5.9.

96

	Expository	Discovery
Structured		
Unstructured		

Figure 5.9. A 2 x 2 factorial design with four cells.

This design is referred to as a 2 x 2 design with four cells. In factorial designs, both treatment or independent variables may be manipulated, but usually in a 2 x 2 factorial design only one variable is manipulated. The manipulated variable (method) is called the experimental variable while the non-manipulated variable (classroom structure) is called the control variable (Gay, 1976).

Main Effects and Interaction

By using the design in Figure 5.9, the researcher can answer these questions.

The first question is: Does the type of classroom organization have an effect upon achievement? It is possible that the students in the structured classroom will learn more than those in the unstructured situation. This phenomenon is known as a main effect. A main effect is the effect produced by the treatment or experimental variable, and it operates independently of the other treatment variable.

The second question is: Does the method have an effect upon achievement? Perhaps one method of teaching is superior to the other method. This is the other main effect.

The third question is: What effect does the interaction of the two variables, method and classroom organization, have on achievement? This is referred to as interaction. It is possible that the students in the structured classroom prefer the expository approach while the students in the unstructured classroom prefer the discovery approach.

Factorial designs other than the 2 x 2 design can be used. Suppose a teacher wanted to experiment with three ways of teaching reading (basal, language experience, combination of basal and language experience) and classroom organization (structured and nonstructured). This design consists of six cells. Main and interaction effects could be studied.

In this chapter many concepts were presented. They included definitions of internal and external validity, factors which jeopardize internal validity, factors which threaten external validity, classical and factorial designs, and symbols. Also presented were concepts dealing with main and interaction effects, extraneous variables, and Stanley and Campbell's four categories of design.

Directions: Complete the following exercises. The answers are given at the end of the exercises.

1. Define internal validity. _____

    _____

2. Define external validity. _____

    _____

3. State how the following could affect the outcome of an experiment.

    a. Effect of history. _____

        _____

    b. Effect of maturation. _____

        _____

    c. Influences of pretesting. _____

        _____

    d. Change in instrumentation. _____

        _____

    e. Statistical regression. _____

        _____

    f. Differential selection of participants.

        _____

        _____

g. Experimental mortality. _____

_____

4. State how the following sources of external
   validity can affect an experiment.

   a. Confounding effects of pretesting. _____

   _____

   b. Interaction effects of selection and
      treatment.

   _____

   _____

   c. Confounding effects of experimental ar-
      rangements.

   _____

   _____

   d. Multiple treatment interference. _____

   _____

5. Is the following a good research design? ___

   Why or why not? _____

   _____

                 X T_2

6. Which of the eight classical designs controls
   for all the sources of internal validity?

   _____

   _____

7. You have reviewed the literature and generated a problem statement. From the problem statement you decide upon a hypothesis. The hypothesis suggests that you administer a treatment (way of teaching spelling) to a group. You decide to pretest before you begin the experiment. Following the experiment, you posttest the students. Which design would you use?

a. _____

   _____

b. Is it a good design? _____ Why or why not?

   _____

   _____

8. You have two groups, an experimental and control. Students are assigned to each group on a random basis. Before you begin the experiment, you pretest. Following the experiment, you posttest. Which design would you use?

a. _____

   _____

b. Is it a good design? ____ Why or why not?

   _____

   _____

9. When would it be necessary for you to use the two groups (E/C), nonrandomized, pretest-posttest design?

   _____

   _____

10. You have decided to determine how a new social studies program affects student achievement in social studies. Because of the situation you are in, you must use the whole class. You administer a posttest only. Which design would you use?

a. _____

b. Is it a good design? ___ Why or why not?

_____

_____

11. You wish to conduct an experiment which has two independent variables - teaching method and intelligence of students. The teaching method variable has two levels - expository teaching and inquiry teaching. The intelligence variable has two levels - high intelligence and low intelligence. The dependent variable is achievement in science. What design would you use?

a. _____

_____

b. Why? _____

_____

12. In a study by Bingham-Newman and Hooper (1974) a variation of the Solomon Four group design was used.

a. By what name does the writer call this design?

_____

b. Diagram the design.

c. What do the authors mean by a variation
   of this design?

   _____

   _____

13. Assume you wish to conduct an experiment with
    two independent variables each with two levels.
    The first variable is a method of teaching
    reading. The two levels are the language
    experience approach and the basal approach.
    The second variable is intelligence of the
    students. The two levels are high and low
    intelligence.

    a. Diagram this experiment.

    b. What kind of a design is it? _____

14. Henderson and Garcia (1973) studied the effects
    of parent training on the question asking behav-
    ior of Mexican-American children. Fifteen
    students were randomly assigned to the experi-
    mental group; 15 were randomly assigned to the
    control group.

    a. What does the term experimental group mean?

       _____

       _____

    b. What does the term control group mean?

       _____

       _____

c. What does the term randomly assigned mean?

_____

_____

15. Henderson, Swanson, and Zimmerman (1975)
    studied seriation training in young children.
    Forty-one preschool Papago Indian children
    from two Head Start Centers in the Papago
    Indian Reservation constituted the sample.
    To which population can the results be
    generalized?

_____

_____

16. Jaus (1978) investigated the effect of en-
    vironmental education instruction on the
    attitudes of teachers toward the teaching
    of environmental education.

    a. What is the independent variable?

    _____

    b. What is the dependent variable?

    _____

    c. If you could select a design for this
       experiment, which design would you use?

    _____

    d. Why? _____

    _____

104

17. A nonequivalent control group design by Campbell and Stanley was used in a study by Merricks and Crocker (1978).

   a. List the book in which this design is explained.

   _____

18. Define main effect. _____

   _____

19. Define interaction. _____

   _____

ANSWERS - CHAPTER FIVE

1. Internal validity asks whether or not the manipulation of the independent variable produced
   the results.

2. External validity is concerned with to what
   population the results can be generalized.

3. a-g. Open

4. a-d. Open

5. No. The sources of internal and external
   validity appropriate to this design are not
   controlled.

6. Number 4 - two groups, (E/C), randomized,
               pretest-posttest;

   Number 5 - two groups, (E/C), randomized,
               posttest only;

   Number 6 - Solomon Four, (E/C/E/C), randomized,
               2 pretests - 4 posttests;

   Number 7 - two groups, (E/E), randomized,
               pretest-posttest;

   Number 8 - three groups, (E/E/E), randomized,
               pretest-posttest.

7. Number 2 - one group, (E), nonrandomized,
               pretest-posttest.

        b. No. Too many sources of internal
           and external validity are not
           controlled.

8. Number 4 - two groups, (E/C), randomized,
               pretest-posttest.

    b. Yes and No. Yes, because all the sources of internal validity are controlled. No, because some sources of external validity are not controlled.

9. When you have to use intact groups because you cannot randomize.

10. Number 1 - one group, (E), nonrandomized, posttest only.

    b. No. Many sources of internal and external validity are not controlled.

11. a. Factorial

    b. This design permits you to study the effects of two independent variables, each with two levels, on science achievement. You can analyze the main effects as well as interaction effects.

12. Solomon Four, (E/C/E/C), randomized, 2 pretests, 4 posttests.

    b.

R	(E)	T_1	X	T_2
R	(C)	T_1		T_2
R	(E)		X	T_2
R	(C)			T_2

c. Open

13. a.

Instructional Treatment (X_1)

| Language Experience | Basal Approach |

Intelligence (X_2) — High / Low

(A 2×2 grid with rows High, Low and columns Language Experience, Basal Approach)

b. Factorial

14. a. The group which receives the treatment.

  b. The group which does not receive the experimental treatment. This group is used for comparison purposes and as such helps to control some of the sources of internal and external validity.

  c. The students were assigned to each group using a systematic process.

15. The preschoolers attending the two Head Start Centers.

16. a. Environmental education instruction. This is the manipulated variable.

  b. Attitudes of teachers toward teaching environmental education. This is the outcome variable.

  c-d. Open

17. a. <u>Experimental and Quasi-experimental Design for Research</u>.

18. A main effect is the effect produced when a treatment variable operates independently of other treatment variables.

19. Interaction is the effect produced when treatment variables interact with one another.

CHAPTER SIX

EVALUATING EDUCATIONAL RESEARCH

Concepts pertaining to the understanding and analysis of research have been presented. Knowledge of these concepts is beneficial to the professional who as a consumer of educational research utilizes these concepts to evaluate or critique educational research. After the student has read this chapter, studied the material, and completed the exercises, he should be able to:

1. Identify the following types of articles: research, essay, and research review,

2. Recall principles of analyzing research,

3. Apply these principles to simulated research studies and evaluate these studies,

4. Apply these principles to actual research studies and evaluate these studies, and

5. Recall in which professional journals research studies are presented.

Professional journals as well as microfiche selections[1] contain many different types of articles. Probably the most common types are essays, research studies, and research summaries.

---

[1] Microfiche selections are copies of articles which are photographed and placed on microfiche. These articles are indexed in Resources in Education.

Types of Selections

An essay is an article in which the author explains how to do something associated with teaching. In such articles the authors might discuss how to make instructional aids, explain how to teach a concept, discuss his viewpoint on a topic, etc. An example of an essay is English's article (1979) on management practice and curriculum leadership.

Another example of an essay is Schrage's (1969) article on multiplication. In this selection, the author discusses a way to present multiplication by using a matrix.

A research review is an article in which the author reviews research on a specific topic. These reviews may be several paragraphs or several pages.

The Review of Educational Research presents a review of research. In the spring 1978 volume a selection by Kearney and Sinclair reviewed research studies pertaining to teacher anxiety. In the same issue Melton discussed research studies dealing with the use of behavioral objectives.

This publication, which is issued four times a year, is a valuable one. In every issue the editors treat different areas. The research in each area is reviewed and summarized. The bibliography which follows each article directs the reader to the source of the actual study.

Some journals reserve space for researchers to present summaries of their research. In Phi Delta Kappan a section entitled "Research Notes" is reserved for researchers who present a summary of their research. For example, Flynn, Gacka, and Sundean (1978) discussed their research on teachers' readiness for mainstreaming and Lufler (1978) discussed his study on discipline. These are not to be mistaken for research studies; these are summaries of research.

Educational Leadership prints a column entitled "Research in Review" on a periodic basis.
These reviews treat topical areas similar to that
format found in Review of Educational Research.
For example, Brent (1974) reviewed research studies
pertaining to operant learning and Cornbleth (1975)
summarized student questioning studies. Reavis
(1978) discussed research studies pertaining to
clinical supervision. These reviews are followed
by a bibliography.

In Today's Education research reviews are
handled in a column called "Research Clues." In
this column the column editor presents a question
and answer approach. For example, in one issue a
question pertaining to basal readers is discussed
(Hollifield, 1979). In another issue the feelings
of parents and teachers are explored with regard
to using calculators in school (Hollifield, 1978).
Both answers are based on a research study. The
source of each study is cited.

These research reviews are useful to the
consumer of educational research because they
present the findings of research in a summarized
manner. A true research study, though, is presented in more detail.

A research study is one which usually follows
a prescribed format. Usually these articles contain such headings as abstract, introduction,
problem, hypothesis, procedure, results, discussion,
and/or implications.

Examples of research studies and where they can
be found follow. This list is not all inclusive.

1. Krey, Netzer, Eye. "Master Contracts of
   Teachers and Supervision of Instruction."
   Educational Leadership, 1977, survey
   research.

2. Chiappetta and Collette. "Secondary Science Teacher Skills I Identified by Secondary Science Teachers." Science Education. 1978, survey research.

3. Merricks and Crocker. "The Influence of Science Process Activities and Selected Science Reading Materials on Reading Achievement of First and Third Grade Pupils." School Science and Mathematics. 1978, experimental research.

4. Sica. "Political Orientation of Mexican-American and Anglo-American Children." Social Education. 1976, survey research.

5. Duffey and Weaver. "Children's Awareness of Watergate, Busing, Energy, Inflation and the Bicentennial." The Social Studies. 1977, survey research.

6. Hirstein, Lamb and Osborne. "Student Misconceptions about Area Measure." The Arithmetic Teacher. 1978, survey research.

7. McMillan. "The Effect of Effort and Feedback on the Formation of Student Attitudes." American Educational Research Journal. 1977, experimental research.

8. Thornell. "Individual Differences in Cognitive Styles and the Guidance Variable in Instruction." The Journal of Experimental Education. 1977, experimental research.

9. Evans and Lovell. "Design Modification in an Open-Plan School." Journal of Educational Psychology. 1979, experimental research.

10. Feldman and Allen. "Student Success and
    Tutor Verbal and Nonverbal Behavior."
    The Journal of Educational Research.
    1979, experimental research.

11. Argulewicz, Mealor and Richmond.
    "Creative Abilities of Learning Disabled
    Children." Journal of Learning Disabil-
    ities. 1979, survey research.

Principles of Evaluation

When a research article has been selected for
evaluation, what principles would be employed?
Listed below are points to consider when evaluating an article. Because the organization and
use of subheads varies among journals, it may not
be possible to respond to all the following.

General Principles
Applicable to All Studies

1. What kind of research is it?

2. Does the abstract contain a brief summary
of the article? The title of the article along
with the abstract should give the reader a good
indication of what the article is about.

3. Does the introduction give background
information concerning the research? Often times
this background information contains work done by
others in the area. Also many times the background
gives the researcher's interest in the problem.

4. Does the researcher indicate the significance or importance of the research?

5. Does the problem statement indicate the
purpose or objective for conducting the research?
The problem statement should be related to the
introduction, that is, the problem statement ought
to be based on the introduction.

115

6. Is the procedure well stated and well organized? The procedure should be an explanation of the steps used to carry out the study.

7. How are the results expressed: Quantitatively or qualitatively?

8. Does the author discuss his results?

Principles Applicable to Some Studies

If appropriate to the study:

1. Is the hypothesis(es) clearly stated? If the heading labeled hypothesis is used, a well written hypothesis must have a relationship to the problem statement because the problem statement should generate the hypothesis or hypotheses.

2. Is the level of significance stated?

3. Are the statistics appropriate to the study?

4. Are the tables presented clearly?

5. Is there a relationship drawn between the results and implications for teaching? Are these logical implications?

6. If an experimental design was used, what factors jeopardize internal and external validity?

7. If the study is a historical one, can the reader determine if the sources cited are primary or secondary?

8. If the study is a historical one, can the reader determine if the process of internal and/or external criticism was applied to manuscripts, artifacts, etc.?

9. Does the research state what sampling

technique was used to select the sample?

10. If any measuring devices such as opinion-
naires or questionnaires are used, does the author
report how valid and reliable they are?

Conclusion

1. Evaluate the overall quality of the study
by deciding if the study is an excellent, good,
fair, or poor one.

EXERCISES - CHAPTER SIX

Simulated Example One

Below are two simulated examples of research studies. Read each and answer the questions at the end of each article.

Abstract

This research was conducted to determine if attitudes of fourth and eighth grade students toward the study of mathematics were similar. The hypothesis generated stated that no significant differences in attitudes of fourth and eighth grade children toward the study of mathematics existed. The results indicate that the null hypothesis was accepted.

Introduction

Some children are fascinated by the study of mathematics while other children despise the subject. These diverse attitudes are experienced by many students in elementary school.

In a study conducted by Jones (1970), he discovered that generally speaking, most elementary school students dislike studying mathematics. His findings also revealed that this dislike seems to become more of a problem as children grow older.

An intensive survey of attitudes of elementary school students toward the study of mathematics was conducted by White (1976). They discovered that most elementary school children liked to study mathematics.

In another study, Smith (1973) discussed that upper level students (grades 6 and 8) stated that mathematics was the least preferred subject in the curriculum. A similar finding was reported in a study of fifth, sixth, seventh and eighth graders by Gordon, (1975).

The evidence from previous studies suggests that there is confusion regarding the attitudes of children toward mathematics. More specifically is the confusion of attitudes between lower and upper level students.

Problem Statement

The purpose of this study is to determine if there is a difference in attitudes between fourth and eighth grade students toward the study of mathematics.

Hypothesis

There is no significant difference in the attitudes of fourth grade students when compared with the attitudes of eighth grade students toward the study of mathematics.

Procedures

Two hundred students took part in this survey. One hundred of the students were fourth graders enrolled in a suburban school; one hundred eighth graders were enrolled in an inner city school.

The mean intelligence quotient of the fourth graders was 95; the mean intelligence quotient of the eighth graders was 115.

The data was collected by using a questionnaire developed by the author. It consists of twenty items which were designed to measure each student's attitude toward mathematics. A Likert scale was used to measure the intensity of feeling of each student to each item.

An attitude score for each student was obtained by adding up the scores for each scale. A score of 20 indicated a poor attitude toward math; a score of 100 suggests a positive attitude toward math.

Both groups were administered the questionnaire
in January. The fourth grade students were given
the questionnaire followed by the administration
of a two hour achievement test in math; the eighth
graders were surveyed the day after a two week
vacation break.

The data was analyzed by computing the mean for
each group.

Results

The mean attitude score for the fourth graders
was 85; the mean attitude score for the eighth
graders was 33. The null hypothesis was rejected.

Discussion of Results

Since the null hypothesis was rejected, it
appears that fourth graders prefer math whereas
eighth graders do not prefer it. This finding is
similar to the one reported by Jones, Smith, and
Gordon.

Implications for Teaching

Since eighth grade students tend not to like
math, teachers ought to present math in situations
which are meaningful to these students. If this
is done, the attitudes of these students should
change.

Teachers also ought to work with the parents
to help improve the students' attitudes toward
math. If the parents are told to insist that their
children complete any homework assignments, this
should help the children to like math.

Finally, the curriculum for eighth graders
ought to be changed. It is obvious that a curriculum which stresses math generalizations and
principles is less effective than one which is
meaningful and relevant to the students.

After you have read the example, respond to the following questions.

General Principles

1. What type of research is this? _____

2. Is the abstract concise? _____

3. Is the introduction to the problem adequate?

    _____

4. Is the significance of the research stated?

    _____

5. Is the statement of the problem given? Is it related to the introduction of the problem?

    _____

6. Is the procedure well stated and well organized?

    _____

7. How are the results expressed? Quantitatively and/or qualitatively? _____

    _____

8. Are the results discussed? _____

Selected Principles

1. Is (are) the hypothesis(es) clearly stated?

    _____

2. Are the level(s) of significance stated?

    _____

3. Are the statistics appropriate to the study?

   _____

4. Are the tables presented clearly? _____

5. Is there a relationship drawn between the
   results and implications for teaching? Are
   these logical implications? _____

   _____

6. If an experimental design was used, what factors
   jeopardize the internal and external validity?

   _____

   _____

   _____

7. If the study is an historical one, can the
   reader determine if the source cited is primary
   or secondary?

   _____

8. If the study is an historical one, can the
   reader determine if the process of internal
   and/or external criticism was applied to manuscripts, artifacts, etc.? _____

9. Does the research state what sampling technique
   was used? _____

10. Does the author report the validity and/or
    reliability of any measuring devices? _____

Conclusion

1. Evaluate the overall quality of the study by deciding if it is an excellent, good, fair, or poor one. Give reasons for your choice.

_____

_____

_____

_____

Simulated Example Two

Abstract

This study was conducted to discover which method of teaching mathematics to fourth grade children, deductive or inductive, was superior. The null hypothesis states that no significant differences in achievement of fourth grade students taught mathematics by using a deductive approach and fourth grade students taught mathematics by using an inductive approach exists. The results indicate that the null hypothesis was rejected.

Introduction

The best way to teach mathematics to fourth grade students has long been disputed. Some authorities in the field have long argued that the teaching of mathematics can be done more efficiently if the teacher uses an inductive approach; others suggest that a deductive approach is better.

In a study completed by Thomas (1963), the experimenter found that fourth grade suburban students learn mathematics best when an inductive teaching strategy is used. In a related study, Paulus (1965), found that fourth grade students learn mathematics best when a "discovery approach coupled with concrete materials" is employed.

123

Other researchers, however, do not agree with Thomas and Paulus. Moore (1967) and Fresno (1969) discovered that fourth grade inner city children learn mathematics best when the "show them and tell them" approach is used. The approach to teaching is primarily deductive in nature.

In an extensive study conducted by Wilson (1970) the researchers concluded that inner city fourth grade students learn mathematics best if a deductive approach is used.

Problem Statement

The purpose of this study is to determine if there is a difference in mathematics achievement of fourth grade students who are taught mathematics in different ways.

Hypothesis

No significant differences exist in mathematics achievement of fourth grade students taught by a deductive approach and those taught by an inductive approach.

Procedures

Subjects. Five hundred fourth grade students participated in this study. Two hundred fifty inner city children were selected to be taught mathematics by using the deductive approach; two hundred fifty suburban fourth grade children were taught mathematics by using the inductive approach.

Design. The experiment lasted four weeks. The inner city children were both pre and post tested using the instrument named below. The suburban children were pre and post tested.

During the four week period (September 1977) the inner city children were taught mathematics 30 minutes a day. The concept taught was the

124

addition of whole numbers (two place) with regrouping. All teachers were trained in using the deductive approach.

The suburban children also receive four weeks (September 1977) of instruction in mathematics. Most of the teachers were trained how to use the inductive approach to teach the subtraction of fractions with regrouping.

During the experiment, the experimenter monitored the actions of the teachers in the inner city schools; the teaching behavior of the teachers in the suburban schools was not possible due to a lack of sufficient time.

Instruments Employed. The pretest used was the Ace Mathematical Concepts Inventory. The posttest selected to measure growth was the Watson Arithmetic Inventory.

Statistical Analysis. The results of the experiment were analyzed in terms of mean gain scores.

Results

The mean gain score for the inner city children was 3.5; the mean gain score for the suburban children was 2.8. On this basis, the null hypothesis was rejected.

Discussion of Results

Since the null hypothesis was rejected, it appears that children should be taught mathematics by using the deductive approach. This approach consists of telling children what to do and how to do it. This approach also emphasized deductive thinking on the part of the students.

Implications for Teaching

All fourth grade teachers should be taught to

125

teach mathematics by using the deductive approach. If teachers are not proficient in such a technique, in service training should be provided.

The results also suggest that pre service teachers receive training in this approach. Colleges and universities ought to institute courses which teach this skill.

After you have read the example, respond to the following questions.

General Principles

1. What type of research article is this? _____

   _____

2. Is the abstract concise? _____

3. Is the introduction to the problem statement adequate? _____

4. Is the significance of the research stated?

   _____

5. Is the statement of the problem given? Is it related to the introduction of the problem?

   _____

6. Is the procedure well stated and well organized?

   _____

7. How are the results expressed? Quantitatively and/or qualitatively? _____

   _____

8. Are the results discussed? _____

Selected Principles

1. Is (are) the hypothesis(es) clearly stated?

   _____

2. Are the level(s) of significance stated?

   _____

3. Are the statistics appropriate to the study?

   _____

4. Are the tables presented clearly? _____

5. Is there a relationship drawn between the
   results and implications for teaching? Are
   these logical implications? _____

   _____

6. If an experimental design was used, what factors
   jeopardize the internal and external validity?

   _____

   _____

7. If the study is an historical one, can the
   reader determine if the sources cited are
   primary or secondary? _____

   _____

8. If the study is an historical one, can the
   reader determine if the process of internal
   and/or external criticism was applied to manuscripts, artifacts, etc.? _____

   _____

9. Does the research state what sampling technique was used? _____

10. Does the author report the validity and/or reliability of any measuring devices? _____

Conclusion

1. Evaluate the overall quality of the study by deciding if it is an excellent, good, fair, or poor one. Give reasons for your choice.

_____

_____

_____

_____

Realistic Application of Principles

1. In a professional journal locate an essay, review of research, and research article. List the source of each. Discuss how they differ.

2. Read several research articles that appear in professional journals. In a two page typed paper, summarize (2-4 sentences) the selection and evaluate the study using the principles discussed.

ANSWERS - CHAPTER SIX

Simulated Exercise One

General Principles

1. This is a descriptive study. More specifically it is survey research.

2. Yes, the abstract is concise.

3. No. Although the author discussed previous studies which have a relationship to the problem, he discusses no studies pertaining to fourth graders.

4. Somewhat. He does state that confusion exists with respect to attitudes toward learning mathematics.

5. Yes, the problem statement is given.

6. No. The use of subheads would aid in the organization of this section. Also note that the collection of data was not similar for each group.

7. The results are expressed in quantitative form.

8. Yes, but only briefly.

Selected Principles

1. Yes, the null hypothesis is clearly stated.

2. No, the level of significance is not stated.

3. No, the statistics are not appropriate. The author does not state what statistical test he used. He reports that only the mean score for each group was computed. If the author wishes to reject or accept the null hypothesis, he should state the specific test that he used

and compare that finding with a predetermined level of significance.

4.   No tables are presented.

5.   Yes, the author does discuss implications for teaching. His implications are misleading for the following reasons:

    a.   Based on very weak evidence he states emphatically that teachers should present math in a meaningful way.

    b.   Nowhere in the article does the author discuss the role of the parents. Yet his second implication discusses this.

    c.   Based on very weak evidence the author suggests that the total curriculum for eighth graders should be revised.

    d.   The author cannot generalize his results to all fourth and/or eighth graders. An improper sampling technique was employed.

6.   An experimental design is not appropriate for this study.

7–8.   These questions are appropriate to historical research.

9.   The author mentions how he selected his sample. Note that the fourth graders were enrolled in a suburban school. Their mean IQ was 95. The eighth graders were enrolled in an inner city school. Their mean IQ was 115. Improper sampling procedures were used to select the samples.

10.   The author does not report the validity and reliability of his measuring instrument.

Conclusion

1. Open

Simulated Exercise Two

General Principles

1. This is experimental research.

2. Yes, the abstract is concise.

3. No, the introduction to this problem is not adequate. The author should present several more studies.

4. The significance of the research is not stated.

5. The statement of the problem is given. The statement is not related very well to the introduction because the problem statement suggests fourth graders in general whereas the introduction to the problem deals with two different groups of fourth grade students.

6. The procedure is well organized. Some factors affecting internal and external validity are apparent. See the answer to question six in the next section.

7. The results are expressed in quantitative form.

8. Yes, the results are discussed, but only briefly.

Selected Principles

1. The null hypothesis is clearly stated. The hypothesis is related to the problem statement, but the problem statement has little relationship with the introduction. See answers three and five above.

131

2. No, the level of significance is not given.

3. No, the statistics are not appropriate. The
    author does not state what statistical test he
    used. He reports only that the mean gain score
    was computed. If the author wishes to make a
    decision concerning the rejection or acceptance
    of the null hypothesis, a statistical test must
    be computed. Also, the result of this test
    needs to be compared with a predetermined level
    of significance.

4. No tables were given.

5. The implications for teaching are misleading.
    In this case the null hypothesis was rejected,
    but the condition for its rejection is based
    on the difference in mean scores and not on
    the basis of statistical inference. Also, it
    would be foolish for educational planners to
    make decisions which affect many people on
    the basis of one study.

6. This study employed the following design:

250 inner city students	T_1	X deductive	T_2
250 suburban students	T_1	X inductive	T_2

    The effects of history, effects of maturation,
    the influences of pretesting and the changes
    in instrumentation do not threaten the internal
    validity because both groups would probably ex-
    perience the same events, mature at the same rate,
    be subjected to the same pretest, and experience
    similar changes in instrumentation. Also,
    experimental mortality is controlled because
    the experimenter can determine who dropped out

132

of the experiment and make the correct adjust-
ment.

Factors which jeopardize the internal validity
include statistical regression and the differential selection of participants.

Statistical regression could occur if one group
is composed of students with high intelligence
and the other group consists of students with
low intelligence. Differential selection of
participants is a source of concern. It could
happen that all of the students placed in the
deductive group knew the concepts before the
experiment started. It is also possible that
volunteers were placed in one group and re-
luctant learners in the other. If this
occurred, volunteers might be motivated to work
harder than non-volunteers.

With regard to external validity the confounding
effect of testing is not controlled because only
500 students out of the population of fourth
graders is pretested. The results are generalizable to only those two groups.

Interaction of selection and treatment is not
controlled. Since the students were not randomly placed in the two groups, to what population
can the results be generalized?

The confounding effects of experimental procedures are not controlled. The inner city
children were taught math 30 minutes a day for
four weeks. The suburban children also were
taught math for four weeks, but the length of
each period and the number of days instruction
was presented is not given. Also, all the
teachers who used the deductive approach
received training whereas only most of the inductive teachers were trained. Finally, the
behavior of the teachers in the inner city

133

schools was monitored; teaching behavior of
the suburban teachers was not checked.

Multiple treatment inference is of no concern
since multiple treatments were not used.

7-8. This is not an historical study.

9.   No sampling technique was used.

10. Questions pertaining to the validity and
     reliability of the tests need to be raised.

Conclusion

1.   Open

BIBLIOGRAPHY

Anastasi, Anne. Psychological Testing. 4th ed.
    New York: MacMillan Publishing Co., Inc., 1976.

Argulewicz, Ed N., David J. Mealor, and Bert O.
    Richmond. "Creative Abilities of Learning Dis-
    abled Children." Journal of Learning Disabil-
    ities 12 (January 1979): 21-24.

Alvord, David J. and Barbara E. Brittingham. "Eval-
    uations Performance on National Assessment
    Objectives." Journal of Educational Research
    68 (October 1974): 59-61.

Best, John W. Research in Education. 3rd ed.
    Englewood Cliffs: Prentice-Hall, Inc., 1977.

Bingham-Newman, Ann M. and Frank H. Hooper. "Class-
    ification and Seriation Instruction and Logical
    Task Performance in Preschool." American Edu-
    cational Research Journal 11 (Fall 1974): 379-
    393.

Bowers, John. "A Flexible Schedule for Hithergreen
    Middle School, Washington Township, Ohio: A
    Proposed Design." Master's Thesis, University
    of Dayton, Dayton, Ohio, 1967.

Bracht, Glenn H. and Gene V. Glass. "The External
    Validity of Experiments." American Educational
    Research Journal 5 (November 1968): 437-474.

Brand, Kenneth J. "Factors that May Affect the
    Passage or Failure of School Tax Levies in Ohio
    as Perceived by Selected Educational Leaders."
    Master's Thesis, University of Dayton, Dayton,
    Ohio, 1968.

Brent, George. "Use of Operant Learning Principles
    in Measuring Behavior Changes in Pupils." Edu-
    cational Leadership 32 (November 1974): 151-154.

135

Button, H. Warren. "Creating More Useable Pasts: History in the Study of Education." Educational Researcher 8 (May 1979): 3-9.

Bybee, Rodger W. "The New Transformation of Science Education." Science Education 61 (January-March 1977): 58-97.

Campbell, Donald T. and Julian C. Stanley. Experimental and Quasiexperimental Designs for Research. Chicago: Rand McNally and Co., 1966.

Chiappetta, Eugene L. and Alfred T. Collette. "Secondary Science Teacher Skills Identified by Secondary Science Teachers." Science Education 62 (January-March 1978): 73-78.

Clifford, Geraldine Joncich. "Home and School in 19th Century America: Some Personal-History Reports from the United States." History of Education Quarterly 18 (Spring 1978): 3-34.

Cohen, Shelby Ruth. "The Relationship Between Convergent and Divergent Thinking in Science as Revealed in Sixth and Seventh Graders." Journal of Educational Research 68 (May-June 1975): 327-330.

Conway, Jill K. "Perspectives on the History of Women's Education in the United States." History, Education, and Public Policy. ed by Donald R. Warren. Berkeley: McCutchan Publishing Corporation, 1978, 273-285.

Cook, David R. A Guide to Educational Research. Boston: Allyn and Bacon, Inc., 1965.

Cornbleth, Catherine. "Student Questioning as a Learning Strategy." Educational Leadership 33 (December 1975): 219-222.

Cronbach, Lee J. and Lita Furby. "How We Should Measure Change - or Should We?" Psychological Bulletin 74 (July 1970): 68-80.

<u>Dayton</u> <u>Daily</u> <u>News</u>, Dayton, Ohio, February 11, 1979,
    12 D.

De Medio, Dwayne L. "Learning Activity Packages in
    French Culture and Their Effects on the Language
    Skills and Attitudes of High School French II
    Students." <u>Journal</u> <u>of</u> <u>Educational</u> <u>Research</u> 72
    (January-February 1979): 169-173.

Doucette, John and Robert St. Pierre. "Anchor Test
    Study: School, Classroom, and Pupil. Correlate
    of Fifth-Grade Reading Achievement." ED micro-
    fiche number 141-418, 1977.

Duffey, Robert V. and V. Phillips Weaver. "Children's
    Awareness of Watergate, Busing, Energy, Inflation,
    and the Bicentennial." <u>Social</u> <u>Studies</u> 68 (July-
    August 1977): 160-164.

English, Fenwick W. "Management Practice as a Key
    to Curriculum Leadership." <u>Educational</u> <u>Leader-
    ship</u> 36 (March 1979): 408-413.

Epstein, Joyce L. and James M. McPartland. "The
    Concept and Measurement of the Quality of School
    Life." <u>American</u> <u>Educational</u> <u>Research</u> <u>Journal</u> 13
    (Winter 1976): 15-30.

Evans, Gary W. and Barbara Lovell. "Design Modifi-
    cation in an Open-Plan School." <u>Journal</u> <u>of</u>
    <u>Educational</u> <u>Psychology</u> 71 (February 1979): 41-
    49.

Fangman, Sister Esther. "The Illinois Test of
    Psycholinguistic Abilities as a Measure of
    School Readiness Determined by a Multiple
    Validity Correlation Coefficient." Master's
    Thesis, University of Dayton, Dayton, Ohio,
    1973.

Feldman, Robert L. and Vernon L. Allen. "Student Success and Tutor Verbal and Nonverbal Behavior." Journal of Educational Research 72 (January-February 1979): 142-148.

Flynn, James R., Richard C. Gacka, and David A. Sundean. "Are Classroom Teachers Prepared for Mainstreaming?" Phi Delta Kappan 59 (April 1978): 562.

Freed, Helen Jeanette Binder. "A Study of the Causes of Reading Failure in the Mad River Township Schools and Some Suggestions for Improving the Reading Program." Master's Thesis, University of Dayton, Dayton, Ohio, 1948.

Fuchs, Gordon E. "A Comparison of the Qualities of an Ideal Teacher as Expressed by Different Groups of Junior High School Pupils." Master's Thesis, University of Wisconsin-Milwaukee, Milwaukee, Wisconsin, 1961.

Fuchs, Gordon E. "The Effects of Three Different Types of Student Teacher-College Supervisor Conferences upon Selected Phenomena Associated with Supervisory Conferences." Ph.D. Dissertation, Ohio State University, Columbus, Ohio, 1974.

Gaver, Donna and Herbert C. Richards. "Dimensions of Naturalistic Observation for the Prediction of Academic Success." Journal of Educational Research 72 (January-February 1979): 123-127.

Gay, L. R. Educational Research: Competencies for Analysis and Application. Columbus: Charles E. Merrill Publishing Co., 1976.

Gesell, Arnold et. al. The First Five Years of Life: A Guide to the Study of the Preschool Child. New York: Harper and Brothers, 1940.

Gesell, Arnold and Frances L. Ilg. The Child from Five to Ten. New York: Harper and Brothers, 1946.

Graham, Sister Francis. "A Study of the Incidence of Cheating Among Sixth, Seventh, and Eighth Grade Children in My School and Some Proposed Remedies." Master's Thesis, University of Dayton, Dayton, Ohio, 1964.

Griffin, Sister Dwyn. "The Historical Background of Four Selected Topics from the Math IV Course." Master's Thesis, University of Dayton, Dayton, Ohio, 1968.

Hall, Elizabeth. "A Conversation with Jean Piaget and Barbara Inhelder." Psychology Today. vol. 3 (May 1970): 25-32; 54-57.

Hammill, Marilyn A. "A Study of Students' Attitudes Toward Mathematics at Saint Mary's High School, Providence, Rhode Island." Master's Thesis, University of Dayton, Dayton, Ohio, 1972.

Henderson, Ronald W. and Angela B. Garcia. "The Effects for Parent Training Program on the Question - Asking Behavior of Mexican-American Children." American Educational Research Journal 10 (Summer 1973): 193-201.

Henderson, Ronald W., Rosemary Swanson, and Barry L. Zimmerman. "Training Seriation Responses in Young Children through Televised Modeling of Hierarchically Sequenced Rule Components." American Educational Research Journal 12 (Fall 1975): 479-489.

Hirstein, James J., Charles E. Lamb, and Alan Osborne. "Student Misconceptions about Area Measure." Arithmetic Teacher 25 (March 1978): 10-16.

Hogan, David. "Education and the Making of the Chicago Working Class, 1880-1930." History of Education Quarterly 18 (Fall 1978): 227-270.

Hollifield, John H., ed. "Do Basal Readers Still Present Stereotypes of Certain Categories of People?" Today's Education 68 (February-March 1979): 10.

Hollifield, John H., ed. "How Do Parents and Teachers Feel About Students' Using Calculators in School?" Today's Education 67 (September-October 1978): 22-23.

Isaac, Stephen and William B. Michael. Handbook in Research and Evaluation. San Diego: Robert R. Knapp, 1971.

Jaus, Harold H. "The Effect of Environmental Education Inservice on Teachers' Attitudes Toward Teaching Environmental Education." Science Education 62 (January-March 1978): 79-84.

Jenkins, Gladys. "Construction of Instruments to Help Teachers Measure Records and Report Progress of Slow Learning Pupils." Master's Thesis, University of Dayton, Dayton, Ohio, 1967.

Johnson, Nancy S. "Selected Creative Activities for Non-Readers in Elementary Special Education Classes." Master's Thesis, University of Dayton, Dayton, Ohio, 1970.

Jones, Robert M. and John E. Steinbrink. "A Survey of Precollege Energy Education Curricular at the State Level." ED microfiche number 155-018, 1977.

Journal Herald, Dayton, Ohio, February 8, 1979, 1.

Kearney, Glenese and Kenneth E. Sinclair. "Teacher Concerns and Teacher Anxiety: A Neglected Topic of Classroom Research." Review of Educational Research 48 (Spring 1978): 273-290.

Kennedy, John Joseph. An Introduction to the Design and Analysis of Experiments of Education and Psychology. Washington, D.C.: University Press of America, 1978.

Kolesar, Sister Barbara. "The Effects of Various Types of Praise on the Self-Concept of a Child in the Primary Grades." Master's Thesis, University of Dayton, Dayton, Ohio, 1973.

Krey, Robert D., Lanore A. Netzer, and Glen G. Eye. "Master Contrasts of Teachers and Supervision of Instructor." Educational Leadership 34 (March 1977): 464-470.

Kuder, G.F. and M.W. Richardson. "The Theory of the Estimation of Test Reliability." Psychometrika 2 (September 1937): 151-160.

Lazar, Irving. "The Persistence of Preschool Effects: A Long-Term Follow-Up of Fourteen Infant and Preschool Experiments." ED microfiche number 148-470, 1977.

Lazerson, Marvin. "Understanding American Catholic Educational History." History of Education Quarterly 17 (Fall 1977): 297-317.

Leahy, Alice M. "The Establishment of a Predicative System of College Success Based on a Study of the 1962 and 1963 Graduates of Meadowdale High School Attending Four Ohio Universities." Master's Thesis, University of Dayton, Dayton, Ohio, 1964.

Lefkowitz, Monroe M., Leonord D. Eron, Leopald O. Walder, and L. Rowell Huesmann. Growing Up to be Violent: A Longitudinal Study of the Development of Aggression. New York: Pergamon Press, Inc., 1977.

Likert, Rensis. "A Technique for the Measurement of Attitudes." Archives of Psychology 140 (June 1932): 5-55.

Lord, Frederic M. "The Measurement of Growth." Edu-
    cational and Psychological Measurement 16
    (February 1956): 421-437.

Luce, Terrence S. and Dale M. Johnson. "Rating of
    Educational and Psychological Journals." Edu-
    cational Researcher 7 (November 1978): 8-10.

Lufler, Henry S., Jr. "Discipline: A New Look at
    an Old Problem." Phi Delta Kappan 59 (February
    1978): 424-426.

Mardis, Verdena Fox. "A Survey to Determine the
    Causes of Failure in the Elementary Schools of
    Montgomery County for 1947-48." Master's
    Thesis, University of Dayton, Dayton, Ohio, 1949.

Marks, Edmond and Charles G. Martin. "Further Com-
    ments Relating to the Measurement of Change."
    American Educational Research Journal 10 (Summer
    1973): 179-191.

McMillan, James H. "The Effect of Effort and Feed-
    back on the Formation of Student Attitudes."
    American Educational Research Journal 14 (Sum-
    mer 1977): 317-330.

McNemar, Quinn. "On Growth Measurement." Educational
    and Psychological Measurement 18 (1959): 47-55.

McTeer, J. Hugh and F. Lamer Blanton. "The Relation-
    ship of Selected Variables to Student Interest in
    Social Studies in Comparison with other Academic
    Areas." Journal of Educational Research 68
    (February 1975): 238-240.

Melton, Reginald F. "Resolution of Conflicting
    Claims Concerning the Effect of Behavioral
    Objectives on Student Learning." Review of
    Educational Research 48 (Spring 1978): 291-302.

Merricks, Anne R. and Robert K. Crocker. "The
  Influence of Science Process Activities and
  Selected Science Reading Materials on Reading
  Achievement of First and Third Grade Pupils."
  School Science and Mathematics 78 (December
  1978): 684-690.

Moore, Kathryn McDaniel. "The War with the Tutors:
  Student-Faculty Conflict at Harvard and Yale,
  1745-1771." History of Education Quarterly 18
  (Summer 1978): 115-127.

Moos, Rudolf H. "A Typology of Junior High and
  High School Classrooms." American Educational
  Research Journal 15 (Winter 1978): 53-66.

Nelson, Lois N. "The Development of Cognitive
  Operations in Young Children." Journal of Educational Research 68 (November 1974): 116-123.

Nevill, Dorothy D., William B. Ware, and Albert B.
  Smith. "A Comparison of Student Ratings of
  Teaching Assistants and Faculty Members."
  American Educational Research Journal 15 (Winter
  1978): 25-37.

Olneck, Michael R. and Marvin Lazerson. "The School
  Achievement of Immigrant Children: 1900-1930."
  History, Education, and Public Policy ed by Donald
  R. Warren. Berkeley: McCutchan Publishing
  Corporation, 1978, 169-197.

Osgood, Charles E., George J. Luci, and Percy H.
  Tannenbaum. The Measurement of Meaning. Chicago:
  University of Chicago Press, 1957.

Ousley, Linda. "A Case Study Studying Second Grade
  Readers' Miscues in Oral Reading Using the Reading
  Miscue Inventory." Master's Thesis, University of
  Dayton, Dayton, Ohio, 1978.

Perkins, Betty Ann. "The Work of the Catholic Sister-Nurses in the Civil War." Master's Thesis, University of Dayton, Dayton, Ohio, 1967.

Pietras, Thomas and Rose Lamb. "Attitudes of Selected Elementary Teachers toward Non-Standard Black Dialects." Journal of Educational Research 71 (May-June 1978): 292-297.

Prah, June Joy. "An Analysis of the Anecdotal Case Histories of Six Failing Second Grade Students with Appalachian Background Enrolled at the Five Oaks Elementary School, Fairborn, Ohio." Master's Thesis, University of Dayton, Dayton, Ohio, 1965.

Pratt, David. "Predicting Teacher Survival." Journal of Educational Research 71 (September-October 1977): 12-18.

Puhak, Sister M. Petronilla. "Reading Aloud to Children: Its Effect on Vocabulary Development." Master's Thesis, University of Dayton, Dayton, Ohio, 1977.

Reavis, Charles C. "Clinical Supervision: A Review of the Research." Educational Leadership 35 (April 1978): 580-584.

Roettger, Doris, Mike Szymczuk, and Joseph Millard. "Validation of a Reading Attitude Scale for Elementary Students and an Investigation of the Relationship between Attitude and Achievement." Journal of Educational Research 72 (January-February 1979): 138-142.

Schrage, Merry. "Presenting Multiplication of Counting Numbers on an Array Matrix." Arithmetic Teacher 16 (December 1969): 615-616.

Schramm, Barbara. "Case Studies of Two Down's Syndrome Children Functioning in a Montessori Environment." Master's Thesis, University of Dayton, Dayton, Ohio, 1974.

Seller, Maxine S. "Success and Failure in Adult Education: The Immigrant Experience, 1914-1924." History, Education, and Public Policy ed by Donald R. Warren. Berkeley: McCutchan Publishing Corporation, 1978, 197-212.

Shaver, James P. "The Productivity of Educational Research and the Applied-Basic Research Distinction." Educational Researcher 8 (January 1979): 3-9.

Sica, Morris G. "Political Orientation of Mexican-American and Anglo-American Children." Social Education 40 (October 1976): 454-456.

Smith, Timothy L. "Immigrant Social Aspirations and American Education." American Quarterly 21 (Fall 1969): 522-543.

Solomon, Richard L. "An Extension of Control Group Design." Psychological Bulletin 46 (March 1949): 137-150.

Stanley, Julian C. "The Influence of Fischer's 'The Design of Experiments on Educational Research' Thirty Years Later." American Educational Research Journal 3 (May 1966): 223-229.

Thorndike, Robert L. and Elizabeth Hagen. Measurement and Evaluation in Psychology and Education. 3rd ed. New York: John Wiley and Sons, Inc., 1969.

Thornell, John G. "Individual Differences in Cognitive Styles and the Guidance Variable in Instruction." Journal of Experimental Education 45 (Summer 1977): 9-12.

Van Dalen, Deobold B. Understanding Educational Research: An Introduction. 4th ed. New York: McGraw-Hill Book Co., 1979.

Vecchio, Robert and Frank Costin. "Predicting
    Teacher Effectiveness from Graduate Admissions
    Predictors." American Educational Research
    Journal 14 (Spring 1977): 169-176.

Williams, Frank E. "Creative Thinking and Person-
    ality: An Exploratory Study of Their Relation-
    ship in Third and Fourth Grade Children." ED
    microfiche number 060-059, 1968.

Wise, John E., Robert B. Nordberg, and Donald J.
    Reitz. Methods of Research in Education.
    Boston: D.C. Heath and Co., 1967.

Yates, F. "Sir Ronald Fischer and the Design of
    Experiments." Biometrics 20 (June 1964):
    307-321.

INDEX

Research, Applied - Types of:

    Descriptive, 5
    Experimental, 5; 10-11
    Historical, 5-6; 43-45
    See also Descriptive Research,Types of

Research Defined, 4

Research Design Defined, 76

Research, Major Types of:

    Action, 11-12
    Applied, 4-5
    Pure, 4

Sample, 59

Sampling Techniques:

    Cluster, 61
    Random, 60
    Stratified, 60-61
    Systematic, 61

Significance, Level of, 26-27

Sources:

    Primary, 45-46
    Secondary, 45-46

Validity, External:

    Defined, 76-77
    Types of:

      Confounding effect of experimental procedure,
        83
      Confounding effect of pretesting, 81-82
      Interaction of selection and treatment, 82
      Interference caused by multiple treatments,
        83-84